# SECRETS OF LIFE

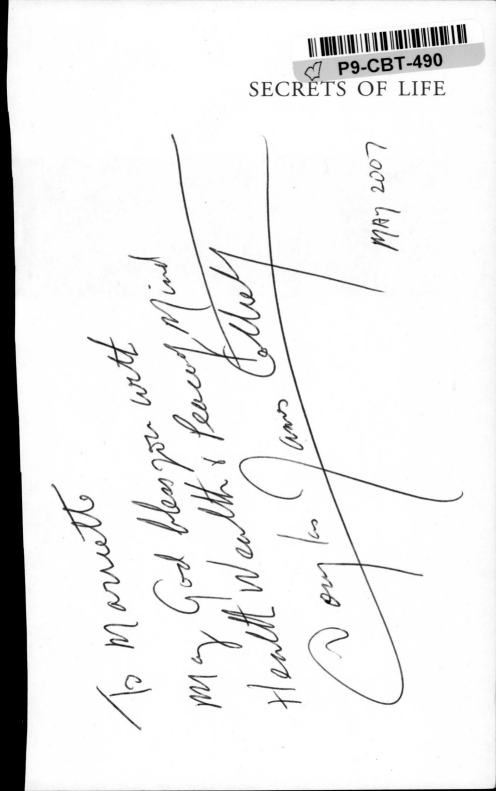

To Morriell

my God bless your with

Health wealth & peace of Mind

I am your fan

[signature]

MAY 2007

# RETS OF LIFE

Unique Insight into the Workings
of Your Soul by the Most Powerful
Intuitive of Our Time

## DOUGLAS JAMES COTTRELL

Compiled & Edited by Douglas M. Cottrell, BA, MA

London, Ontario, Canada • www.douglascottrell.com

Many Mansions Press
London, Ontario, Canada

ISBN 0-9735067-0-9

Cover design by Douglas M. Cottrell.

*First Edition*

*Printed in Canada*

*FOR KAREN*

*"No man is an island, entire of itself;*
*every man is a piece of the continent, a part of the main.*
*If a clod be washed away by the sea, Europe is the less,*
*as well as if a promontory were,*
*as well as if a manor of thy friend's or of thine own were:*
*any man's death diminishes me,*
*because I am involved in mankind,*
*and therefore never send to know for whom the bell tolls;*
*it tolls for thee."*

- John Donne, Chapter 17,
*Devotions Upon Emergent Occasions*, 1624

# FORWARD

## By Robert Appel, BA, BCL, LLB

Having leafed through a considerable number of spiritual and meta-physical tomes in my half-century-plus of living, I can confidently opine that this astounding work is a thoroughly remarkable, one-of-a-kind effort.

My sense is that the first-time peruser will be immediately captivated by the firm-but-gentle "tone" which, ultimately guides the patient reader to the extraordinary vantage point at which Truth and Illusion can irrevocably, absolutely - and finally - be distinguished, one from the other.

For those of us on a quest to better understand where we have been - and, even more important, where we are heading - this modest and unprepossessing volume may ultimately prove itself to be the "barber's barber" of its subject niche. Years, even decades, from now, *Secrets of Life* may well turn out to be the "gold standard" by which all other works of its kind will be judged.

This is no small claim, nor is it made lightly.

Pause for a moment to consider that the essential thrust of *Secrets of Life*, the meat if you will, is that most of the hard Science you have been taught since High School isn't really that 'hard'...and most of what you have come to accept as Reality isn't quite that 'real.'

Which, in turn, raises the question - how did Douglas James Cottrell first happen upon such a profoundly esoteric, and thoroughly vast body of knowledge in the first place? How did he become so gracefully proficient, so effortlessly confident in areas of Spirituality and MetaScience which have, at one time or another, baffled even the greatest sages and thinkers of our Epoch?

*And there, indeed, lies a tale within a tale.*

Quietly, and with almost no fanfare, Cottrell has, since the early 1970s, been perfecting a rare form of spiritual practice believed to be of the most ambitious tenor ever attempted by modern man. Boasting a direct lineage to the lost arts of the ancient Oracles of Delphi; and best known more recently (within the last one hundred years, or so) as the "Edgar Cayce Phenomenon," Cottrell has, for over three decades, and on over 25,000 individual occasions, demonstrated the extraordinary ability to bypass the mid-level (or "conscious") mind - and connect directly to the High Self, or God-Mind.

That accomplishment is nothing less than the "pre-conscious psychic disposition" that the great philosopher Carl Jung first postulated; the "Universal Unconscious" in which all knowledge is stored - and from which, provided you have proper access, all knowledge can, with proper technique and intent, be successfully retrieved. That you, kind reader, may never have come across Cottrell's work previous to this is merely a testament to this great man's wisdom in ensuring that, while still a young adult raising a family, demand for his most unusual skill might never actually exceed supply - to the point where 'premature' fame or fortune would have, perhaps, confounded his ability to best serve those with 'first dibs' on his love and devotion.

Still, even in the absence of notoriety or fanfare, and with only word-of-mouth as his ever-faithful publicist, truth-seekers from across the globe have patiently sought out Cottrell for his unusual "talent," day-in and day-out, for well over thirty years. (Trivia buffs and potential Cottrell biographers take note that the largest ongoing foreign demand for Cottrell's "sessions" has arisen, consistently, from Japan. Cottrell himself has never been to Japan, nor does he speak a single word of Japanese. And, for those with a mathematical bent, it is also worth considering that, within his own lifetime, Cottrell's body of work has by now out-matched Cayce's, in terms of total sessions done, by a factor of about 2:1).

Still, we must not get ahead of ourselves!

Like all really good books, this one should be judged by its impact on you, and your own personal future - rather than by an exposition of its past, however unique. So, please, don't dally. Lean back, turn the page, and enjoy the journey.

This is indeed a very special book, from a truly extraordinary individual. The least you can expect from this work is that it will change your life. The most you can expect is that it will totally transform it.

*- Robert Appel, BA, BCL, LLB*
*Toronto, Canada*
*March 2004*

# CONTENTS

# INTRODUCTION

### Douglas James Cottrell

On the surface, my father, Douglas James Cottrell appears to be an ordinary, uncomplicated, good-natured and friendly family man. He enjoys the simple things of life: driving in the countryside, grooming horses, walking the dogs or playing hockey with his friends. He and my mother, Karen, have been happily married for thirty-six years and have four children. They live in an average, quiet suburban neighborhood in London, Canada. To the casual observer, he is an unremarkable man. But as the saying goes, still waters run deep. For beneath the plain and ordinary surface lies an intuitive ability so powerful and accurate that it staggers the imagination and challenges our very notion of what it is to be human.

### Biography

Douglas was born in Toronto, Canada in December 1949 to Thomas and Elinor Cottrell, an average, not overly-religious working-class couple who struggled to make ends meet. The eldest of four children, Douglas split his youth between work at the family wood-yard and football games at Central Technical High School. In 1965 he fell in love with Karen Paquet, and they were married in February of 1968.

**DOUGLAS JAMES COTTRELL & KAREN COTTRELL**

# INTRODUCTION

Douglas had taken a job as an apprentice, and was soon working as a full-fledged pressman for the nation's largest daily newspaper, *The Toronto Star.*

In July of 1968, Douglas and Karen became parents and their lives were forever changed. The birth of a child, especially the first child, should be a blessed event. But for the young couple, the arrival of daughter, Cheri-Anne, was little short of traumatic. Delivered weeks overdue, Cheri-Anne collapsed shortly after being born. Medical staff resuscitated her several times. Over the weeks and months that followed, Cheri-Anne was in and out of hospitals. She was prone to convulsions. Doctors put her on medications to sedate her. By age two and a half, Cheri-Anne was diagnosed as severely mentally and physically retarded. Douglas and Karen finally acquiesced to the medial advice to place her into an institution, resigned to the medical opinion that she had only a few months to live.

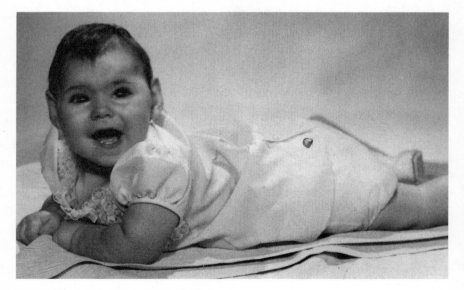

**CHERI-ANNE COTTRELL, Toronto, Canada, 1968**

# INTRODUCTION

Douglas and Karen refused to give up hope for Cheri-Anne, and they continued to pray to God that their daughter's life could be spared. In 1975, their prayers were answered. Douglas had been working in his workshop, when suddenly he had a strong feeling - an urging - to turn on the television. As he did, the screen filled with the image of a man who appeared to be talking in his sleep. He was describing in great detail the health problems of someone else, and - more importantly - he was explaining what could be done to remedy them. This sleeping man was Ross Peterson, a "medical intuitive" who practiced a form of deep meditation that was popularized by 1930s American intuitive Edgar Cayce. At that moment, Douglas knew there was hope for his daughter, and he and Karen determined that they had to see this man.

A very pragmatic and down-to-earth person, Douglas had always been skeptical and dismissive of psychics, tarot card readers and palmists. Karen's Catholic upbringing had taught her that fortune telling was sinister. They had never been to a psychic before, nor had they explored any unorthodox or alternative form of treatment for Cheri-Anne. Needless to say, their optimism was tempered with much fear when they met Peterson.

They did not know what to expect when they approached Peterson's hotel room that fateful day, and they were extremely anxious and apprehensive. Their fears were quickly laid to rest, however, as for the first time in seven years, someone was able to intelligently articulate how Cheri-Anne came to develop in the way that she did. Moreover, Peterson was able to explain what steps could be taken in order to bring Cheri-Anne back to health. He recommended natural treatments that were foreign to Douglas and Karen, such as chiropractic and massage. He also suggested various foods and herbs to be given to Cheri-Anne that would act as remedies for her traumatized body.

Peterson's recommendations not only saved Cheri-Anne's life, but they opened Douglas and Karen's minds to a larger world. For Peterson had revealed to Douglas that he, too, had an aptitude for deep meditation, and he encouraged Douglas to explore his own intuitive abilities. Douglas told Karen that he had to find out for himself if this were possible. In his words, if he was able to "help just one child" (as Cheri-Anne had been helped by Peterson), then the efforts would be well worth it.

Over the course of many months, Douglas not only learned to develop his innate intuitive abilities to the level of his instructor, but he soon surpassed him. Like Edgar Cayce, Douglas had the gift of true insight. Teaming up with his family doctor and chiropractor, Douglas began his experiments into testing the power of his intuition. Word of Douglas's ability spread quickly. As more and more people sought out his guidance, he discovered his true calling. Acting on faith, he quit his job at *The Toronto Star*, giving up financial security to invest all his time into metaphysical research and the nurturing of his spiritual abilities. For in his mind, what job could be more important than helping his fellow mankind? In his thirty years as a metaphysical researcher, intuitive counselor, teacher and lecturer, Douglas has helped thousands of people the world over. He has been tested time and again by the general public, business executives, journalists, medical doctors and scientific researchers. His ability is genuine. He has proven himself to be the most powerful living intuitive of our time.

## Deep Trance Meditation

*"It is like having one foot on earth, and one foot in heaven."*

*- Douglas James Cottrell*

He lays back in a reclining chair, closes his eyes and begins to breathe deeply. Within minutes, Douglas has entered the state of Deep Trance Meditation (DTM). It is as if his conscious mind has moved out of the way, fading into the shadows and allowing his contemplative mind (or what may also be called the soul mind) to come forward. The contemplative mind is the consciousness of the immortal human soul. Unlike the rational mind (or personality mind), the contemplative mind is not bound by the physical restraints of time and space. As part of the universal consciousness of mankind, it sees all, knows all, and understands all. Where the rational mind is finite, the contemplative mind is infinite.

Communication between the rational mind and the contemplative mind takes place when the rational mind is receptive (i.e. during altered states of consciousness such as dreaming, meditation and hypnosis). When the body is excited, agitated or stressed, it demonstrates the ability of seemingly superhuman physical strength and speed. Similarly, when the body is profoundly relaxed, the mind becomes capable of seemingly superhuman mental feats: clairvoyance, clairaudience, clairsentience, precognition, premonition, and prophecy.

As its name implies, DTM is a very deep, trance-like state of meditation, a state some have described as the "twilight state between consciousness and sleep" (also termed by others as a self-hypnotic or sleeping state). In this altered state of consciousness, Douglas's respiration and heart rate are slowed, his blood pressure is lowered, and his brain activity changes (a condition medically referred to as "theta level"). The ability to consciously relax his body and become emotionally detached from the physical, sensual world is something Douglas learned to do over many years. He believes that, to varying degrees, this is an ability that everyone can learn to express as well. Most everyone, he says, has experienced some degree of intuitive or spiritual phenomena in their own lives (i.e. premonitions, déjà vu, visions, gut feelings, prophetic dreams, etc.).

### Mind Projection and Remote Viewing

There are people who are so amazed and awestruck at the mental ability that Douglas exemplifies that they simply cannot believe it. The degree of accuracy and amount of detailed information that comes through during a DTM session just seems impossible. Consider the following:

*"Beginning in the uppermost portions of the body, there is in the neck both severe compression and mild rotation, approximating an S-curve, affecting the seventh, sixth, and third cervical vertebrae as well as the Atlas-Axis. The head is sitting crooked on the neck. Blood flow to the upper areas of the cranium is somewhat restricted, causing mild oxygen starvation. Brain activity is generally sluggish, especially affecting the reflex areas and motor skills centers. Vision is deteriorating noticeably in the left eye and painful sensitivity to bright light is also developing. Some hair loss as well, affecting predominantly the scalp area to the front and to the right side. Nasal passages are clear and the tissue forming the lining is healthy. Gums and teeth are normal. Moving now to the chest cavity...."*

It is as if Douglas is reading a report on a patient, but what is actually happening is that he has "sent" his contemplative mind to scan a client hundreds of kilometers away and report back an overview of the health condition. As stated previously, the contemplative mind is infinite and is not bound by time or space. For Douglas to report of the minutiae of health detail - even to the cellular level - of someone across the world from him may seem impossible, but it is something he does with great skill and uncanny accuracy almost every day.

In an effort to explain this phenomenon, scientists have dubbed this ability as "Remote Viewing." In a way, it is as if Douglas projects his mind out of his body to some remote distance (or even to some remote past or future time) to examine some person, place or object. Douglas himself has described it in another way, however. He says, "Picture yourself as a dot. Now picture an energy field surrounding this dot. This field extends so far out that it collides with the energy fields of other people." Douglas describes the space where the energy fields overlap as the place where truth and illumination resides, for this is a demonstration of the contemplative mind.

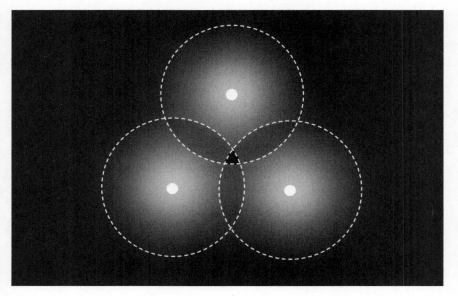

# INTRODUCTION

## Practical Spirituality

If it offers no practical use in daily life, then information has little value. These are words Douglas lives by. He learned to practice DTM for one sole reason: to help others as he and his family had been helped by a genuine, reliable intuitive source. Douglas's own unique branch of practical spirituality has offered comfort, insight, and understanding to thousands of people over the years: parents grieving the loss of a child, young people wondering what action they should take, and people trying to comprehend the injustices they see around them. What is right and what is wrong?

As accessed by Douglas during countless DTM sessions, the contemplative mind articulates the spiritual realm, and the spiritual laws that govern our souls in terms that make it accessible to everyone, regardless of their level of education, background or their religious faith. Time and again it has reiterated that each of us possesses a soul. We are, in effect, spiritual beings living in physical bodies in this physical world. The world we live in - especially the world today - can be very confusing, clouding the judgment of even the most pious among us. How can we learn to operate in an enlightened, spiritual and harmonious way in the chaotic world we live in? What is right and wrong behavior? What are the consequences? Why do bad things happen to good people? How can we all learn to live in harmony? These are the questions that matter the most - the spiritual questions, the questions of right living, proper action and the meaning of life and the nature of God itself. Why are we here? The contemplative mind knows the answer.

Witness for yourself Douglas's amazing ability not only to demonstrate the vastness of human mental and spiritual potential, but also to tap into this limitless resource of knowledge and understanding. The chapters that follow are taken from direct transcripts of several DTM sessions by my father conducted during the summer and fall of 2003. They were transcribed verbatim by my sister, Louise, along with Sheila Gatis and Diane Petis. I edited the transcripts, cleaning up the diction and grammar, where needed. As much as possible, I attempted to stay true to the sessions themselves. Because of this, you may notice some repetition of concepts, phrases and motifs between the various chapters of this book. I trust you will find such recurrences as helpful in reinforcing certain ideas. If you find them redundant, then feel free to skip over them. This book is offered in the hope that the wisdom of my father's words will bring you as much inspiration, enlightenment and comfort as they do to our family.

I wish you all the best and all of God's blessings: health, wealth, and peace of mind.

*- Douglas M. Cottrell,* BA, MA
*London, Canada*

# Chapter One

# THE THREE STATES OF MIND

The world we live in, the material, physical world, is both a world of duality and a world of extremes. Likewise, there are two extremes of states of mind: the contemplative and the rational.

### *The Rational Mind (or Conscious Mind)*

The rational mind (also known as the personality mind, logic mind, or intellectual mind) is concerned with this physical dimension, or the material world. The rational mind is concerned with all aspects in an earthly, materialistic way. It deals with the laws and activities of the world and governs your nature or personality (and, to some degree, that of the subconscious mind: its values, opinions and material beliefs). It is of the egocentric self, whereas the contemplative mind is of the enlightened, ever-present self. The contemplative mind represents your high self, and all your spiritual qualities and abilities. It is that part of you that is immortal, and which attempts to seek to do the greater good. It aspires to return from whence it came and reunite with God (or the God-head or the Christos).

*The Contemplative Mind (or Super-subconscious Mind)*

Also known as the upper mind or soul mind, the contemplative mind is the sum total of all you have been, are now and will be. It is the larger "I am." It is eternal and, in actuality, is the essence of you. It is that part of you that is of God and from God - your soul.

The contemplative mind is capable of communicating beyond the bounds of material time and space. It also has the ability to communicate with other minds to which it is sent, to which it has some interest, or to which it deems as being meaningful. It is able to touch upon the "ever-present moment." In that moment, everything exists in a present state, a state of ever-present, continuous understanding - a sort of timeless view of everything that has been, is now and will be. The more you engage in this dimension or state of mind, however, the less interested you become in the physical world. The contemplative mind is like the Hindu Elephant Mind: direct, slow moving, and powerful. In contrast, the rational mind is like the Monkey Mind: chaotic, scampering, changing direction, changing values, changing destination. It goes all over, without order.

*The Subconscious Mind*

The subconscious mind acts as a facilitator between the rational and contemplative minds. The subconscious mind has no values. It knows neither right nor wrong, nor does it have any concept of direction. It only understands those things of which it is told, directed or informed. For instance, if you repeat the phrase "I am not sick. I am not sick. I am not going to be sick. I am not going to be sick. I am not sick," the subconscious mind takes only the value "sick." While the contemplative mind understands the intention of the statement, it is unable to redirect the subconscious mind (for it is like a five-thumbed helper). The value of sick, planted in the subconscious mind, results in the physical body taking this direction and becoming sick.

### How States of Mind Relate

The conscious mind is influenced by the emotional states; the contemplative mind is not. You can think of the contemplative mind as an older version of you: a parent or grandparent. Likewise, the rational mind can be likened to a rebellious youngster: independent, stubborn, obstinate, and prone to throwing tantrums when the higher self or contemplative mind wishes to intervene to do what is best for you.

Therein you have the struggle between the rational mind and the contemplative mind. The contemplative mind is a creative, passive, greater mind. The rational mind is an independent, active, disturbing, random mind. When planted in the contemplative mind, a creative seed manifests intentions, desires or thoughts initiated in the rational mind. Attitude helps form the thought, desire or want in the rational mind. The contemplative mind ensures that all that is held in the rational mind is brought about in the physical world.

### Fountain of Thoughts

Ask yourself these questions:

*Where does thought come from?*

*How is thought produced?*

*How is it that a stream of thoughts can be linked together?*

*Why is it that thoughts occur at certain points of time rather than others?*

*What is the cause of a thought being produced?*

*What triggers a thought to be born into existence?*

# CHAPTER ONE

The contemplative mind is like an ocean - an ocean of thought. The rational mind, being like a trigger or disturbance, allows a thought to bubble up from the depths of the deep water of the contemplative mind, breach the surface and, like a fountain, be expelled into the air above for a short time. It is the collaboration between the rational mind and the contemplative mind which allows the welling up of this fountain or spouting of thoughts - or even the simple emanation of one thought - out of the ocean.

The subconscious is the force that allows this to occur. Emotions and attitude are the ingredients to form a thought. Where do inventions come from? Inventions are, in fact, remembrances of things that have already been created. Science makes new discoveries each and every year, but the reality is that scientists only come to understand a thing that has existed in nature forever. A scientist attempts to harness this knowledge and use it for his or her own ends, but in essence, like the ocean, what he or she comes to "discover" has always existed. The only new thing is the person who came to the conclusion or witnessed the observation. It is new to him or her.

To understand the power of the contemplative mind, therefore, remember that the contemplative mind has always been, is now, and always will be. It is the creative force in which all of creation resides. The rational mind allows a sequential, linear approach to understanding the contemplative mind. But being a lower mind (or the small "I am") the rational mind is a finite mind. The contemplative mind is an infinite, ever-expressing, ever-expanding mind. It is very difficult – in fact, impossible - for a finite mind to understand the infinite.

Simply, put, the contemplative mind, then, is a discerning

mind (demonstrating the ability to discern), whereas the rational mind is a discrete mind (expressing the ability for discretion). The contemplative mind is the creative force within you. It is that part of you that gives life, creates life and is life. Within this part of your mind are all the aspects of your soul - the so-called "spiritual abilities" or gifts: the ability of the mind to have control over physical matter, the demonstration of telekinetic ability, prophetic vision, and so on. All are demonstrations of this ever-present contemplative mind. Indeed all the spiritual gifts, abilities or talents are within the repertoire, evidence, and activities of your contemplative mind.

On the other hand, all finite abilities, and everything that must be examined in a finite way (such as logic, intellect and reason) are part of the rational mind. The rational mind is based on a person's knowledge, education, beliefs and their value system, whereas the contemplative mind may be *magical* in its masterful creation of manifesting a miracle or some other thing that is unfamiliar to the rational mind. But the rational mind is superior in organizing the creative forces in a linear way.

### Accessing the Contemplative Mind

Let us back up for a moment. The judgment and criticism of the rational mind or personality mind is such that memory and emotion are attached to it. These attachments tend to taint your opinions of what you consider truth. The contemplative mind has no such difficulty, for it is not adulterated or affected by emotions. Therefore your higher self can look very truthfully at your lower self, for your lower self may be a little jaded and biased, and this may color your daily responsibilities or actions. The contemplative mind does not experience such things. There is simply the naked truth. There are no secrets. There are no lies. In the contemplative state of mind, everything is out in the open. Now this tends to frighten the rational mind, which believes it can hide things it knows to be wrong, harmful or selfish. The rational mind may have the perception that it can be secretive and hide in the darkness, but the contemplative mind is exactly the opposite. It perceives all and perceives the light. And this is what all who aspire to spiritual enlightenment tap into.

The manner in which you can touch upon this higher state of mind is by entering into "the holiest of holies" - the deeper states of meditation - and through prayer. As the part of you that exists forever, the contemplative mind is the aspect of you that engages or exists in the dimensions beyond the physical world: the spiritual planes of consciousness. It is, therefore, governed by rules of the spiritual planes. It is hard to believe that the spiritual realms have rules or limits, but conditions do indeed exist (see chapter six for further discussion).

Again, this higher self is without emotion, save for the ever-present emotion of unyielding and unconditional love. It is from this perspective and to this consciousness that all who pray for guidance, assistance or some benefit should do so. For the assistance, benefit or prayer is answered by the soul mind or contemplative mind itself. However the veil of pretense, disbelief or sense of being unworthy or undeserving tends to negate this communication from the low self to the high self. For instance, some say "I believe in God," and "I believe that all prayers are answered." They then pray for a million dollars and immediately say, "And I hope I get it." By saying this, they have voiced their disbelief, which instantly negates their prayer. The high self, therefore, does not pay attention. Understand that prayer is simply a state of thinking - continual thinking - and what is thought about is believed. The stronger the belief, the more vital and possible is the manifestation of the prayer in the physical world.

The contemplative mind has the ability, the power, or the force to create things instantly. This is the aspect that heals your body when it is in difficulty, or when it is sick. It is also the part that greatly changes your physical body to a state of well-being, almost instantly (i.e. it performs miracles). While this is the part of you that has that ability, it is your *expectation and attitude* (in the rational mind) that determine whether or not it will happen. You can unwittingly be the saboteur of your own prayers.

### Access Through Dream States

The conscious, rational mind requires the subconscious mind to be the liaison between itself and the contemplative or soul mind. Thus, the subconscious mind is like a conduit or tether between the two aspects of mind. During sleep states, the conscious mind "moves out of the way" and the subconscious mind "becomes" the personality mind, if you will; that is, the sum total of all your beliefs, concerns and values. The contemplative mind, then "becomes" the subconscious mind, with wisdom and benevolent thinking. It becomes a parental self. During dream states, the contemplative mind will manifest or bring into your life what the subconscious mind can accept.

The subconscious mind is formed or directed under the control of the conscious mind. During sleep states, what was held in the mind during the day, when the body was awake is worked upon. This includes your worries, fears, excitements, contemplations, expectations of reward, and determination to advance or be successful. All that is held in your mind during the day – the good and the bad - is transferred through the subconscious mind to the contemplative mind. In turn, the contemplative mind produces them in your life, causing the challenges and rewards of life to be put in your path.

Accessing this in a state of sleep is not as good or controlled as in the states of meditation, however. But during sleep it is automatic. The personality mind goes to rest and the contemplative mind becomes more directive or in control. Like a parent guiding a child, allowing the child to take his or her own steps or choose a direction (without too much interference), during altered states of consciousness, the high mind directs the low mind from a point of wisdom. During dream states, meditative states, or states of vision, your mind leaves your body and examines other far-off dimensions, or seeks the counsel of those minds from whom it would expect information and who are of some interest in observing your life: its teachers, guardian angels, or spirit guides.

Times in which the body is unconscious are also an opportunity for you to touch upon the contemplative mind. However, in a state or delirium or under the influence of narcotics or alcohol is not the preferred or recommended way. You may touch upon the higher self, but it would largely be useless or inappropriate.

### Trance and Hypnosis

Then there is the self-induced trance: a state of being consciously aware but allowing the subconscious mind and the contemplative mind to be in harmony. This is seen in a variety of ways in which the body can possess super-human strength or is able to endure what would appear to be physical pain. In essence, it is the high self or contemplative mind completely in control of the low self or conscious mind. This is a state of mind that is induced in a "waking sleep," similar to what is seen in aboriginal peoples of the world who have discovered the ability to set aside their conscious mind and enter a state of trance. You also see this demonstrated in people who become hypnotized or mesmerized. Properly done, you may touch upon the higher states of mind, briefly, in hypnosis as well as in trance.

### Group Consciousness

Where there is a gathering of many people with a holy person, great healings occur. For the contemplative mind of the one hooks up or conjoins with all others in the room. As such, the force of one is multiplied by the force of the many, and that one who is the focal point - the master of ceremonies, the preacher or the speaker on stage - is, at the same time, a receiver, a transmitter and a generator of great power, or great creative force. And this person has the ability to focus or direct this creative power. This, therefore, is a demonstration of a multiple approach or connection to the contemplative mind. It is usually witnessed in charismatic healers or religious ceremonies, but it is also done in theatres or music concerts as well: same effect, different expectation.

### Summary

The rational mind, therefore, is independent, isolated from all, determined to be its own director, and determined to be isolated. The contemplative mind on the other hand, is like a drop in the ocean - each drop singular in its essence, but indistinguishable from the whole. During the states of trance, dream or meditation, the finite mind becomes part of the whole. It is like a single drop of water returning to the ocean. In its own consciousness, its own limiting way, it is still an individual drop. But, in essence, it becomes part of the whole body of water. As the ocean would touch upon all the shores of the world, so does that drop immediately have that same ability, you see.

# Chapter Two

# GOD

There is a longing in every soul to understand God and to be reunited or repatriated with God, for there everything is perfect. Our souls are of God and from God. As such, all of us share a need and desire to come close to God. The human mind, however, cannot comprehend God, for a finite mind cannot comprehend the infinite. God (or the God-head, or the Christos), that which existed in the beginning is infinite and omnipresent. It is a consciousness that transcends time and space. It can be finite as well as infinite at the same time.

To comprehend the nature of God, however, is to comprehend something that you cannot see, that you only have evidence of its existence, and that when you come close to it, great things happen. God is like electricity. It is unseen. It comes in many forms. There is no doubt of its existence, for you see the results of its existence. You cannot handle it, for if you do, you will die. You cannot contain it, but you can make it appear in small, finite ways. Yet it is infinite and exists in all material things. Electricity can be used for creative purposes and for destructive purposes. God is the creator of all things, and also the great destroyer of all things. Without electricity, virtually nothing can exist, for electricity at the cell level causes a vibration to emanate, exist, or be contained within the center of a cell. And, yet, electricity can go through all things, animate and inanimate, including the planet and all beings, animals, plants, insects and everything else that occupy it. Like a lightning bolt of electricity, God reaches down from the heavens above, and man reaches up from the earth below.

To comprehend the spiritual aspects of God, understand that God is a force and also a mind. Actually, God is an accumulation of many minds, and yet is of one mind. Each and every person possesses a fragment of God – the soul. The consciousness of the soul (or the soul mind or contemplative mind) is in unison, connection or communication with all other soul minds at the same time. The finite, ordinary, human consciousness does not recognize, see or understand this, but it is, nonetheless, a fact. God, therefore, is an accumulation of all souls. Yet the souls which are perceived to exist in the physical world and in the dimensions beyond it are but a part of the whole.

## Separation of Souls from God

There came a time when a large segment of souls broke away from the mass or unity of souls that we call God. This separation was the original sin of separation, and it was done when each soul was given the gift of free will and free choice. For God is such that God loves each and every soul - so much, in fact, that God gave them such a gift as free will and free choice. Those souls which separated *chose to do so*. You can consider them "rogue souls" which, in their vanity, left the protection of God and the home they knew forever. They migrated out into physical matter. Through temptation and adulteration of their essence or their perfection, they absorbed mass and became dense. They lost their way. They became ingrained in physical matter too much and for too long. Like a drunkard who loses his way, loses his consciousness and forgets, ingrained in the physical world, these souls became intoxicated with the carnal and material aspects and the spirit of forgetfulness overcame them.

However, God is a loving and just God. God would have none suffer - save for those who choose to do so. Therefore, a pathway, mechanism, or way back to the God-head was created. However, God, in its infinite wisdom, is such that each soul who wishes to be repatriated from whence it came must undo all that it has done in the first place. This is a process often called "self meeting self." You must overcome the temptations, adulterations, desires and wants that keep you apart from God. When you do this, then you will have attained some form of perfection and are, therefore, warranted, allowed and welcomed to return to perfection itself. And until you do so, you may arrive at various spiritual levels or stages of consciousness to work upon, contemplate and overcome the inadequacies of yourself. *All souls must do this.*

### God as a Loving Parent

The nature of God can be understood as the emotion of love; a love so perfect and so complete that it overwhelms all inadequacies, difficulties, and transgressions. It is, in fact, unconditional love so pure that it allows each and everyone to exercise their free will and free choice - for their own betterment or to their own detriment. Consider a child learning how to ride a bicycle. The child is determined to do so, even though there is some danger involved and potential for injury. But the child's parents love their child so much that they allow him or her to do whatever he or she wants. They attempt to school and pre-pare the child so that they can release him or her into the world. Thereafter, the child lives life totally responsible for his or her own actions and deeds – good, bad, or indifferent. Likewise is the nature of God.

## Moving Toward God

When you work with God, you are a procreator or co-creator. When you work against God, however, it is as if you are standing in a dark room, void of all assistance, totally responsible for your own actions. Your spiritual progression is totally determined by your own blindness and the actions you take in this dark room. This is why it is said that *when you turn your back on God, God's back is turned on you.* But when you beseech God, God's benevolence is offered without reservation or condition. For God's nature is such that God is wise. Only at such time when your soul achieves this understanding can you move for-ward, increasing your awareness and enlightenment. The spirit within yourself – your soul - causes this recognition to occur in the first place, for the spirit of humans tends to influence us to move away from pain and towards the peace or pleasure we long for. People are motivated by material or carnal aspects to improve themselves or find a better way. However, God is so loving and forgiving that the rules of advancement are very plain. You must go through your soul as if peel-ing an onion, removing the layers that have parted you from God.

## God is Love

Therefore, the nature of God is love: all love; love that is perfect, omnipresent and omniscient. For only through love can all things come to be as they should. Only though perfection and love can you return to the God-head. As the nature of God is love, in order to come close to God, you must learn to love as God would. Throughout history, there have been teachings to love your neighbor as you would love yourself. In essence, this commandment is the crux of all other commandments so that you might return to God. In so loving another as you would love yourself, would you not forgive the other, should he or she stray, no matter how far or how horribly? Would you still love the other if he or she achieved great things, or would you become filled with jealousy, spewing criticism and judgements upon the other, further separating you? In loving the other as you would love yourself, you would understand tolerance and patience. Through experience, you would gain wisdom. This is the pathway to God. This is the nature of God. There are no injustices in the universe, as you know it, for God is a loving and just God, filled with compassion, and dispensing love that is pure so that you may become part of the whole and experience - in yourself - the essence of God.

### *"If God is With Thee, Who Can Be Against Thee?"*

When you are standing up to the strong when they are in the wrong, when you are standing up for the sake of righteousness; when you are doing what you think is right (and you know for certain that your actions are beyond you and for the greater good); when you are avoiding temptation; when you are attempting to avoid wrong-doing or evil; when you are attempting to be for all good, then, indeed, are you not on the side of God? For God is justice. God is correctness. You must behave correctly when you are near or around God. Why? Because God is perfection.

The phrase, "If God is with thee, who can be against thee?'" was coined to rally those people who are attempting to do good in the world. If you are attempting to be God's servant, to do God's service, to do God's work, and to attempt to be a co-creator, in removing darkness from the world - even minutely - then God is, of course, with you. When a child aspires to do great things, his or her parent does not go in front of the child, but becomes supportive of the child, knowing full well that the child must move forward on his or her own cognizance and responsibility. Likewise, God would encourage, furnish, deliver, cause, or affect those situations which allow you to accomplish what you have determined to be right and for the greater good. Those who would attempt to destroy you, overcome you with hardship, slander your name, or harm your body cannot stand in their shame and darkness in the blinding light of God.

God stands for right. God is the creative force. If you have aligned yourself with this, then, indeed, you are aligning yourself with the purpose of God. Understand there is a plan so that all souls can return to the original point of departure from God: the point that is perfection. Understand that when God is with you, you will have great support from all the creative forces that would rally to your aid. For it is the purpose of all souls who have gone before you and have found their way back to the God-head to encourage their younger brothers and sisters (so to speak) to follow in their footsteps. Thus, they would aid you with all you need to overcome darkness and to overcome those poor and misguided souls who attempt to bring darkness into the world. If God is with thee, none can be against thee, for there is no greater force in the universe than God. No misguided soul who resides in dimensions beyond the physical world can stand the perfection and brightness of God's light. Therefore when you align with God, you will not suffer influence on any dimension beyond the physical world; nor would you suffer any inadequacy or lack in the physical one.

When you attempt to stand up to the strong when they are in the wrong, when you attempt to stand up for the sake of justice, or for the betterment and welfare of any and all others, then you invoke the greatest force of all. There is no greater force than God. Who possibly could stop you from doing God's work? God's work is taking care of each other, as if you are taking care of yourself, bringing the world to a higher vibration or greater understanding; in essence, a place of great love.

Belief is built on evidence that is manifested in the physical world. Through this evidence, and this belief, faith is built. Only as evidence is experienced over and over - as doubt is erased, and as faith is strengthened - can you come to believe that God is with you - and therefore no one can be against you.

### *Where is God?*

When you speak of the spiritual dimensions beyond the physical world – a place where God, miracles, and such exist – think of it as the place where electricity exists: in some unseen, far-off place. In reality, however, electricity is under your very feet right now. It is within your body. Every time you move, you create electricity. Every second, electromagnetical influences occur in your brain, your body, and all that is about you. God is the same.

The dimensions that you believe are beyond your physical self are not far-off; they are within you, just outside of you, and beyond you at the same time. You are in a natural state, existing in harmony with God, just like you are with electricity. Has it not been said *"God is within me, and I am within God"*? Like electricity within and without, if you are, indeed, a part of God, God is not far away. God resides within your heart. *The only difference between you and God is that you do not know who you are.* If you knew who and what you were, then you would know that God is within you, and you are within God. There is no separation or isolation, for you are a living soul inhabiting a physical body. You conjoin with all other spiritual aspects, minds, beings, souls, ghosts, angels, guides, ancestral influences and immortal souls - the God-head itself. You are part of the whole, and yet you are separate. You are electricity yourself.

Comprehend who and what you are, in this regard, and you can see that you are not alone, that you are part of the whole. Like electricity that is everywhere, so are you. Again, the only difference that separates you from God is your knowledge of who you are and what you are - of the God that is part and parcel of you. Look within your heart. The purpose of physical life is to awaken your inner self, to demonstrate your spiritual aspects while in this physical body. Overcoming temptation and excess allows you to spiral up and return to the God-head itself. From the microcosm to the macrocosm you exist. The only need is to know yourself and to look into your heart. There you will find all things. It does take some strength to do this. For when you look upon yourself, you do see all aspects of yourself, good and bad. Look for the light that is within you, and, indeed, you will have found God.

# Chapter Three

# MIRACLES

## What is a Miracle?

When there is disease in the body one moment, and then the disease has vanished in the next, some would say that a miraculous healing has taken place. A miracle is generally perceived as some event that is unsolvable or unchangeable; something done without any process, somewhat "magically." It is generally regarded as having the great hand of God upon it - and, indeed, it can be perceived as that, for how else could it be that someone with a great physical deformity is instantly transformed into perfect health? The finite mind cannot understand this. But could such a healing simply be an acceleration of the natural occurrences of the body? When someone cuts an arm, normally it takes three days for a scab to form and the scar to be healed. What if the process could be sped up from three days to three seconds? Miracles are, indeed, such a process.

Matter is controlled by thought. Matter does not automatically "know" what to do. Matter needs a thought form to direct it. When matter is controlled or directed by a thought that is so powerful, so ordered and so knowledgeable, cells of a broken bone will virtually align themselves or direct themselves to be replaced, replenished and healed. How is this possible? At the atomic level, all things are merely little particles floating around. At some level, most solid objects are not solid, but hollow, for there is space surrounding the atomic structure. When there is an order or direction at the atomic level, all matter simply lines up, joins up, or becomes one again in perfect unison; for what appears to be solid is not. However it takes a great consciousness, great control, and a great mind to direct that thought to make such things happen.

Miracles, therefore, are the end result of both the purification of the matter and the purification of the thought. Combined, they control the matter to change itself into perfection (or for a sick or injured part of the body to become healed). Damaged cells may become irregular in shape or unharmonious. A miracle causes them to be in harmony, at peace, and to return to their normal vibrational rates. The particles of a broken bone or damaged tissue can instantly rearrange themselves so that they fit together again and the vibrational rate is either slowed down or sped up to the normal vibration - and likewise healing occurs. From a practical, small perspective, this is the concept of miracles.

### Awareness at the Cellular Level

But understand when you appeal to God and the creative forces, disease is very little. It is simply that which should not be. Disease is simply being "ill-at-ease" with what is natural, correct or perfect. For perfection and growth are of God. Miracles remove the dis-easement and re-establish ease, the end result being healing. But somewhere in there is a command or direction of thought which affects the very cells themselves. For understand that cells have a consciousness. When disease comes into the body, the consciousness of the cell can be masked, forgotten or misdirected. You might say the cell is blinded. When the disease is removed, the cell's consciousness returns to harmony, associating with other cells. This awareness at the cellular level causes cells to be regenerated in their original, perfect state with proper vibration, consistency, and materialization. Typically cells grow, live a life and are then terminated and discarded. It is possible, however, for cells to keep the same frequency of vibration from the beginning. This would perpetuate the cell and the new cells to maintain their perfection for a long time.

You see, miracles influence cells similarly. For the mind is the builder and the mind is the way. What is held in the mind is manifested in physical form, both in yourself and in others. If there is a great unity of minds focussed on a single thought, then the thought becomes so great that the consciousness of the damaged cell is raised to its normal vibrational rate and to a state of perfection or healing. Instantly done, a miracle occurs. God, the angels, and any other interested souls may also be called upon or summoned to intervene or assist in the relief of pain and the healing of a physical body. But it is to the contemplative mind or soul mind of yourself that you should first appeal for intervention and assistance in your life.

### Miraculous Manifestations

A miracle can also be the instantaneous appearance of some object - food or some other matter. There are exemplifications of this by holy people throughout the ages, and even into the present day. All things can be reduced to the same thing - a particle, an electron, ash. All things take form from a state of mind or a thought. An orange has the understanding or the thought that it will become an orange long before it is a seed. The consciousness is contained within the seed to not only produce an orange but to produce all the physical aspects prior to producing an orange (such as the tree). An orange will never become a mustard plant or a rock. It becomes what is held within - the thought or consciousness. Understand this and you have a glimpse not only into the consciousness of the cell level and the creative forces in all things, but also of the importance of thought in the creative process. In the production of an orange, as well as in the production of all material things in your life - including the healing of bone or the removal of disease from your body - there first must be a thought. It is just a matter of getting your body to work cooperatively to use all the healing processes within it in a single, purposeful direction. When this process is sped up to such a degree that it appears to occur instantly, then you consider it a miracle.

### *Miracles as Evidence of God*

As a soul, you are of God and from God. All creation is of God, is it not? When the contemplative mind or soul mind is appealed to for the performance of some miraculous event, the end result is often attributed to the work of God. This is fine, just as all evidence of electricity can be contributed to electricity. Electricity is everywhere and yet it is nowhere. It is seen in running a motor, a huge machine, or even a factory. All things that are the result of electricity are related to electricity itself. It is usually not considered that way. Electricity is considered more as a light switch on the wall or a light bulb in the ceiling. You forget all that is behind these exemplifications of the great force and power being used on the small level but still existing on the greater level. Similarly, those who do not understand that they are all part of the sum total of what makes up God may attribute miracles to God, even though they had a hand in the miracle themselves. They made prayers for intervention, or held thoughts for assistance in their own minds from other individuals, or they overcame conditions of self meeting and forgiving self. All of these are exemplifications of the great creative force that is within all of us – the soul mind or the contemplative mind - and, in that way, are exemplifications of God. But do not doubt that your creative mind - the contemplative or soul mind - has no role to play. Your soul is of God and from God, and, as such, is a part of God.

# Chapter Four

# DEATH, THE PRE-EXISTENCE AND POST-EXISTENCE

### Physical Death

What is physical death? Simply put, it is a choice. At the end of some number of years of physical life, your soul simply moves out of your body, giving up the flesh. It is the reverse of what happened at the beginning of physical life when it originally inhabited the body. Understand that your soul can – and does – leave your body for short periods of time, particularly during deep states of sleep or deep states of meditation. However, during such times there is a "tether" between the soul and the body (sometimes referred to as the "silver thread," or "silver cord"). This tether allows the soul to find its way back to the physical body, as it would sojourn through the different dimensions beyond the physical world. During the state of physical death, however, there is no cord attached.

At the moment of phyiscal death, the soul, being somewhat apart from the makeup of your physical being, simply vacates the flesh. During this process, the body appears to succumb to a kind of sleep-like state, but in actual fact, the body is going through a number of chemical and physical changes. Respiration ceases, heart activity ceases, and the body drifts into a state of coma or deep sleep. At this point, there is a "collection of the soul." The soul usually resides in and around the heart area. The soul migrates to the pituitary and pineal glands (a.k.a. *The Church of Philadelphia*) and then it exits the body from the head. A soul can alternatively choose to exit from the solar plexus, which is sometimes considered the main entry point of the soul.

As the body deepens its inactivity or relaxation, the soul actually expands out of the body before it is collected. In other words, it has a feeling of floating or levitation. There is a separation that occurs between the rational mind, the subconscious mind, and the contemplative mind. At the point the body goes to sleep, there is still a cognizant awareness of what is taking place. It is the same awareness one experiences while in a dream state. If there is a willingness to embrace physical death, this separation usually occurs without any pain or difficulty. There is a feeling of wonder and euphoria, a sense of being surrounded with warmth and great unconditional love. Then there is the sensation of moving through a tunnel, or moving past streaming lights. When the soul has exited the body, there is an awareness of the next dimension beyond but there is also an awareness of the place from which the soul has just come. Usually the soul flees from the body. Not too often is there an attempt to re-enter it, for usually the body is decrepit, aged and in disrepair.

It is as if a huge weight has been lifted, and there is a sense of complete and utter freedom and ease of movement. There is also the overwhelming feeling or sense of being surrounded by great love. This is what awaits all when they leave behind the physical body.

# CHAPTER FOUR

## *The Dimension Beyond*

There is no need to fear some darkness or ghoulish reality after physical death. It has been put into the minds of humans that death is to be feared and that there are states of hell and damnation that exist beyond the physical dimension. The reality of the next dimension is completely different, however. In that dimension, as your soul becomes aware of the feeling of love, it also becomes aware of others who are waiting to welcome it to the next dimension: some would call them angels, spirit guides, ancestors, or way-showers.

The time after physical death can best be described as a time in which some education of the soul and some healing are necessary. The soul is presented with familiar images that help with the transition. As the rational mind or personality mind is still thinking in worldly terms, those things that appear to it will be, of course, worldly. For the personality mind continues on for several days (and, in some cases, for several years), but eventually its attachments, familiarity and logic of how the world works soon fade and evaporate. The life it has just experienced becomes remembered by the soul without any emotional attachment (as all previous lives are remembered). It becomes just one more experience of the soul.

With the conscious mind gone, the subconscious mind now takes its place and directs the contemplative mind. In the next dimension, the subconscious mind, and the evidence of the physical world that has been recorded upon it, similarly has no emotional attachments. Therefore you might consider it as a very matter-of-fact level of consciousness, without fear, anxiety, enthusiasm, or anticipation. There is simply the realization of where it is, what it is doing, where it has been and what it has done.

When the body dies, the soul is not left alone. It is met by somewhat of a "welcoming committee" of souls. As physical death occurs, the soul is immediately taken for healing and consultation so that a spirit of forgetfulness can come over the soul. The personality mind - filled with all the emotional states from physical existence - can fade away, be put asunder, and be put on the record of the physical life. Then the soul can move on to the level of spiritual awareness at which it wishes to arrive. To do this, the soul first progresses through a healing center and an educational center.

### Soul Healing

This healing level is an in-between dimension. It can be visualized as a hospital-like setting or healing center where doctors and nurses aid the sick and injured. Trauma, murder, accidental death and violent death are usually the causes for souls to pass into this realm. Those who die lonely and depressed, those who regret taking on physical life, or those who pray for death because of overwhelming emotional strain also find themselves in this healing place. Those souls who are of a higher mind and are higher developed care for these poor, misguided souls. Once there has been a "nursing back" to a proper understanding, and the trauma or derogatory experiences of physical life have been healed, then the soul can migrate on to the dimensions that lie beyond.

### Soul Education

Those souls which journey from physical death to the next dimension and arrive with expectations - whether of heaven or hell, nothing or something - whether they be Atheist, Buddhist, Hindu, Christian,

Muslim or any other religion - will arrive at a place that can be considered the educational center. Here the physical life that was just experienced is recounted, examined and explained. This process helps the soul to ascertain what level of consciousness it has achieved, and what dimension it wishes to enter next (let us use "higher" and "lower" for simplicity, but there is no such judgment in this dimension). For each soul arrives at the level for which it has knowledge, or is capable or deserving, based on its spiritual progression or advancement. If you have a great understanding of the spiritual world while here in the physical world, this understanding will assist you in the afterlife to help you go to the higher dimensions – those which are closer to God.

The soul arrives at a point of like-mindedness, for on the spiritual levels, like attracts like. Picture this level as a place where like-minded souls (or more exactly, souls which share a common "pattern") gather in groups. Those who have a tendency toward philosophical understanding, for example, would arrive in a dimension in which there are philosophers. They would stand in groups of three or more, conversing with each other, developing the philosophy from their experiences in the world, their knowledge of beyond the world, and their experiences throughout time as a soul. Those who have an aptitude for teaching would find themselves in a dimension where teachers congregate. Regardless of pattern, like attracts like. The souls all congregate in these areas or dimensions, so that they might go over the lives just lived, and plan their next lives for their spiritual progression. For in these dimensions, a soul selects its next incarnation. It moves beyond its current consciousness and "graduates" to a higher level.

The cycle of reincarnation continues until the soul ultimately becomes experienced through all aspects of physical life - so much so, in fact, that it loves the world and experiences itself fully throughout the world. When this happens, there is no need for the soul to return to the physical world again. Those who achieve this level of spiritual enlightenment are self-realized and fully-realized beings. During their last incarnations, they usually choose to return to the world fully aware of their consciousness as God-like beings in a physical form. These people are regarded as avatars, saints, miracle-workers, and great spiritual leaders. They enter in this form in an attempt to raise the consciousness of humankind to a higher level – one of uncondi-tional love or oneness with God. For the original sin was the sin of separation. All who have entered the physical world had, at one time, separated from the God-head (that point from which all souls came). Using their free will and free choice, they found their way into the world. When the souls found the world such that it is, they decided to return from whence they came.

Understanding this, you can see why it is necessary for souls to go through the different dimensions and the different levels of con-sciousness that exist in the world: so that they might fill themselves with all consciousness, all understanding, and all knowledge. Only when this is done, however, can they move to the higher levels, or return from whence they came. Souls came into physical matter for selfish experiences. Through temptation they became trapped in the material world, becoming less and less aware of their spiritual home-land. They turned to the dark side of the temporal or corporeal worlds, but at some point of misery and loneliness, they decided to turn around and return to the point of origin: the God-head. For that reason, they need to go through the different strata to arrive back home.

## *Earth-bound Souls*

Now those souls who become earth-bound, or those who get caught up in their misguided ways (some may call evil, lustful and violent ways) also have places where they are "assigned." They are so much engrained in the material world and physical experiences that they continue on in their minds in the physical world, haunting a house, a property, or a place. For in their minds, physical death has not occurred to them. They have simply moved out of the body and continue on in a pretend way, as if they were still alive. Their personality mind or rational mind persists and they continue to exist in a twilight world, a world of ghostly experiences. They appear as a translucent image. They look the same, dress the same and carry on if they were in daily life. If a staircase had existed in their time and had since been removed, they would still walk up the staircase, for it would still exist in their minds. It is a state without time. For them, hundreds of years may pass by in the twinkle of an eye. Even though they have long been dead, their souls still believe they are physically alive and they continue to reside in their old homes. They still have a consciousness and an association or attachment to their material possessions. Filled with jealousy, when a new owner comes into the house, on occasion they become enraged at the "invasion." People have perceived this rage as the mischievous activities, feelings, sights and sensations associated with hauntings.

Those who are earth-bound - those who you would hear of as ghost hauntings - are simply those souls who do not know to move on. These souls do not have to remain earth-bound forever. Sometimes they become aware that they are physically dead. At such time they look up and see a shining light and feel the sense of overwhelming, unconditional love. Then they are drawn up into those places of education or healing and they move on.

In a similar way, there are individuals who have had such traumatic experiences in life that they are resentful of having to come back into the physical world again. They resist with all their will and might and must be assisted back into physical life. This is usually done in order for the soul to overcome the trauma and emotion that has been so engrained in its consciousness. For it is the purpose of souls to take on the flesh again and again so that they may learn to love the world with all their hearts and minds; loving it so much so that they can put it aside and move on to the next level of consciousness or their next stage of evolution.

### Other Earth-bound Souls

Souls which arrive at dimensions filled with a mischievous or evil consciousness do so only because this is what they believe existence is all about. They must go through these dimensions until they come to such a point of despair and loneliness that they would finally look up and say "My God, help me." For in these dimensions, murderers are attracted to murderers. Those who seek power for selfish means – political tyrants, murderers and usurpers - have their own level of consciousness and they must reside here, for it is their understanding of how things are. These types of souls have an attachment to the world as well. From time to time, they seek to "invade" or possess the body of another. When a body has become inebriated or subdued by drugs, it can be more easily taken over. Usually these mischievous and misguided souls enter into living bodies for only for a brief time. When they do, they may experience the emotion of fear, or of dominance over another, or rage. In this way, they may remain earth-bound and attached to the world for a brief time or for long time. It is up to the individual soul. As with the case of other earth-bound souls (or ghosts), they continue existing in this way until they come to that point of despair. Only when their awareness is increased and they move away from isolation, misery and evil towards those souls who are constructive, unselfish and good, then they may move on toward a higher dimension of awareness.

### Planning and Preparing

Therefore, if you are prepared for death, and you willingly approach death expecting to see cheery cherubs in the dimensions that lie beyond, you can ascend very quickly at the point of physical death to a higher level of consciousness. Those who share this perspective willingly look forward to physical death, as they consider it their spiritual rebirth or their return to the place from whence their spirit came. For them, death is a sort of going home, leaving this temporal playground or school yard to move into their eternal home. There they exist for all time in the ever-present moment. With varied degrees of ascension, they ascend higher and higher into a state of love that is pure, complete and unconditional. And not only can this be aspired to and touched upon in physical life, *but it should be*. At the moment of physical death, how you understand death - if you fear it or accept it - affects your arrival on the different spiritual planes or dimensions.

Death should not be seen as a dark and evil thing, for it is merely the completion of a cycle. Your soul originally existed in the pre-existence, then it went through life in the physical world. It goes back into the post-existence when it gives up the physical world. The pre-existence and the post-existence are essentially the same. The post-existence is a healing period during which the soul can forget and move on from its current personality and its associated emotions – anxiety, fear and wonder. The freed soul can then move into the pre-existence, a period in which the planning of its next life is made. For in the pre-existence, the soul selects and plans its next physical body. It also chooses its family, physical abilities and certain circumstances and events that it wishes to experience in life. Sometimes a soul makes an association with other souls. They agree to come into physical life at the same time in order to help one another experience what they have selected to experience. These helper souls may come into the world as teachers, co-workers, friends, family or parents. While each comes with its own agenda, they come into the physical world in such a way that their agendas merge or match. In working out this plan, each of the associated souls guarantee that as they take on a new physical life, they would be able to meet their "co-workers" and be able to work out the karma, plan, or experiences in association with each other. These same souls are those who wait for you in the post-existence. Whether they are siblings, parents or those who are simply meaningful to you, they will be there again when you move on from this physical life to help you put together all the experiences of your life for your progression. Once again, they go over the experiences for the purpose of making a choice so that they might decide when, where and how to re-enter the world (if this is what suits them). This may be done in a group, in a pair (as soul-mates) or individually.

## *Choosing a Hard Life*

Those souls who plan heinous crimes and horrific experiences - both as a victim and as a predator - may be on the same "planning board" in the pre-existence. Think of it as a case of one, great soul willing to go through a life of misery or suffering in order to help another soul overcome its need for violence or dominance. For one soul may need to experience what it is like to be a predator, as well as the life-long guilt and shame that also goes along with it. Or a soul may need to feel what it is like to be incarcerated for fifty years. Keep in mind that the soul mind or contemplative mind needs these things to add to its own record for its ultimate benefit or progression. There is no judgment. There is only a willingness to help those souls who are lesser to rise to a greater level of consciousness. It does take a great soul, therefore – usually someone who has lived many lives - to "give up" a life in order to help another progress in its spiritual sojourn in this way. But the subconscious mind has no emotion - no fear, no anxiety – save for a sense of love and compassion. Thus, it is willing to make such a sacrifice. This is usually the sign of a great soul. Look to those people who have come into the world as examples - as religious leaders, as those who helped human-kind advance to a greater level of brotherly-sisterly love. Have they not suffered great physical pain? Have they not suffered shortness of life? Have they not lived a life of torment, torture, challenge, imprisonment and then physical death? If you examine the lives of the disciples of Jesus, you will find that all but one suffered horrendous deaths. If you examine the life of Mohammed, you will find that he had to flee for his life because of his beliefs. Moses himself, a great leader, suffered greatly and lost all his position and wealth. He became a leader of a tribe of people who, in the end, challenged his authority and rebuked his goodness or his gift of freedom. Look at Krishna, and others who have come along: they have given up all things in the world, so that there may be an advancement of human-kind towards love. Leaders come into the world and they follow a path of long-suffering (whether in public, or in families, or in organizations). Long-suffering demonstrates the willingness to - through example - lay down your life and make some contribution for the advancement of others. The mark of an advanced spiritual being is the willingness to take on physical flesh so that *others* may find their way home again.

Physical death, then, should be considered both a surrendering or letting go of the earthly, corporeal things that you value and an embracing of a higher value or a higher understanding as you enter the spiritual dimensions beyond. For as you feel in the physical world, you feel in the spiritual world. The only difference is that, save for love, all other emotions are left behind. Like the rational mind or personality mind in the corporeal world, they fade away in the spiritual world. Therefore, aspire to love. To die is to know unconditional and pure love.

### *Young Death: Why People Die Young*

Why do some people live to an old age while others die young? The short answer is primarily because it suits the purpose of their souls. The soul has a measured time to experience physical life for its express purposes. Whether it is two hours, two days, two years, two decades, or ten decades, the soul itself reckons how much time it wishes to spend in the physical world in a certain body, circumstance, or environment.

Now this is the generic answer. Reality is, of course, much more complicated than this. Some people may wish to give up life simply because they do not like to be in the physical world. Some people shorten their lives at their own hand. Others fail to take care of their bodies and experience diseases which cause a premature end to their lives. Those who are wise, however, and experienced, closer to the God-head, realize the privilege and the importance of taking on physical life. They do not waste the opportunity. Is there truth to the saying "Only the good die young?" Perhaps. But who can question why a soul chooses to exit physical life when it does? Life is short. Live life to the fullest.

### *Communication with the Deceased*

Consider the following example: a woman is killed in a car crash, leaving behind her children. Does a parent - who has great love for her children in physical life - automatically abandon those children in the afterlife? No, she does not. The parent watches over the children from a vantage point in the spiritual dimensions – the astral plane. From here, she can help to arrange things for her children and protect them as a guardian angel. The parent might appear in dreams or visions when the child is in a deep state of sleep or meditation. And during this time, the earth-bound soul of the parent can directly communicate to give the child advice or direction. They cannot, however, interfere in the free will of the child.

For souls who have left their physical bodies are still resident in an in-between plane of existence known as the astral plane. It is certainly possible for those in the physical world to communicate with those who have moved on from it. Should a soul, such as the soul of a parent, have the will to do so, it can communicate with any it wishes to, provided the living person is in some receptive state of mind (i.e. an altered state of consciousness such as meditation or sleep).

During sleep states, your soul may leave your physical body to communicate with another in this in-between dimension. Mediums and psychics who demonstrate that they can communicate with the dead enter an altered state of consciousness to accomplish this. One should exercise caution in doing this, however. A deceased parent communicating with his or her child is a different matter than one who is reaching out into the ethers seeking contact with any soul who happens to be "floating by." Keep in mind that earth-bound souls tend to bring into their communication their own personalities. People who practice automatic writing, dowse with a pendulum, play with a ouija board or use any other source that reaches out into the unknown run the risk of coming in contact with mischievous souls looking to feed on fear. Like vampires, they feed on the emotional disharmony or fear that they can generate in people who have unwittingly contacted them.

People who are trained to do so are able to select to go directly to the higher levels or states of mind. Here they may call upon the souls of great avatars, leaders, historical figures and others for assistance or intervention in some difficulty or problem. They may also call upon their ancestors to assist them, for do not ancestral relatives have an interest in the present-day family? Of course they do, for it is their lineage, closeness or kinship. So, in summary, it is quite possible for a medium to reach out and speak to the dead, but it is also possible for ordinary people to reach out to deceased friends, relatives or some other person of significance. This may be achieved while in dream states, vision states and states of meditation. For in these states, your soul can touch upon the soul of your deceased relatives, your guardian angels and souls with which you worked out some plan in the pre-existence. You can even touch upon spiritual icons such as Jesus, Buddha, or Krishna, as well as avatars and saints. Those who have died are simply souls who are beyond the physical or corporeal world. They still exist. They are still willing to enter into the physical world and give assistance, if they have a mind to. But practice caution when attempting to communicate with the dead. Mischievous souls should be avoided, for they simply cause havoc in the world.

## *Dealing with Death*

We have all experienced the death of a loved one - whether a family member, friend or some other person we hold meaningful to us. Everyone has experienced grief when a loved one dies. Grief is a natural - although selfish - emotion. You grieve because you believe you have lost something. You think that you will never see your loved one again, and that you will never again be able to talk to him or her. Missing your loved one and enjoying him or her is fine, for your grief is a demonstration of how much love and affection that he or she generated. But do not despair, for your loved one will return as soon as he or she knows how - or as soon as he or she is able to - from the dimension of the healing center and educational center. Then, while you are receptive, in a state of dreaming or meditating, he or she will come to call upon you to show you that he or she has been liberated from bearing the hardship of physical life and has been made whole again in the spiritual realm. During these states, communication can occur, reassurances can be given, and reassertion of contact made between yourselves. You are not alone.

Also understand that the physical, corporeal world is a world of hardship. The spiritual world is one of immortality, filled with love. Understand that you have been left behind by your loved one because you may have some task or purpose yet to be fulfilled. Therefore, you should get to it right away. Do not despair for the deceased person, for he or she will watch over you. And it will only be a few, short years before you will join up again. Then, when your time comes to enter the dimensions beyond, he or she will appear before you as part of the welcoming committee to take you to your next level of consciousness.

Therefore, do not grieve, but feel joy. Release the soul of your loved one into *the real world* that exists beyond this physical, corporeal one. In doing this, you'll come to the understanding of just how much better off the deceased person is in the dimension of love. You are the one who is left behind, faced with certain challenges, responsibilities, and lessons still to be learned. Those souls who have gone on beyond would grieve for you, who must still remain behind.

It is the choice of the soul to move beyond the physical world or to stay in it. There are many who have gone to the higher levels of consciousness and have touched upon the face of God, yet they returned. They do so by their soul's own free will and free choice. Keep in mind that this life is but one breath in the life of your soul. As the soul lives forever, there is no need to believe that you have lost something when a loved one dies. What if this particular life-time allowed your friend to move on to the highest level of consciousness possible? What if you have helped serve that purpose? Then you would see the death as an honor. What if it was necessary that your spouse went on first, in order for you to learn to take responsibility and demonstrate what you have learned from your spouse? Then this would be a blessing. If you could only remember what it is like in the dimension beyond the physical - the ever-present moment, or the pre-/post-existence, surrounded by unconditional love - then you would understand what a wonderful state this dimension is. Each of us must go through what our souls decided to go through. Each of us must advance on our own responsibility. In fulfilling our duty, we earn the right to aspire to the greatest or highest level of consciousness.

When a loved one dies, realize you are never alone. As you get on with your life, look for guidance from above. Your loved one who has gone beyond will be by your side as much - and as often - as he or she possibly can. There is no darkness. There is no night. There is simply love and light. Choose what you wish to choose, but we would suggest light and life.

# Chapter Five

# REINCARNATION

As the name implies, re-incarnation is a re-entering into the flesh; it is taking life as a human being (once again) to meet those things that your soul must meet while in the flesh. When you physically die, there is an in-between place where your soul goes prior to entering into another body. Physical death, therefore, should be thought of as a rebirth of your spiritual self into a body once again. The process, therefore, is an on-going cycle of physical life - physical death - spiritual life - spiritual death.

## *The Purpose*

Your soul, therefore, has a purpose for entering into a body in the way that it does. Over many lifetimes, you would incarnate in different cultures, and in different parts of the world. You would also switch genders, switch roles, and switch social standing so that, in the end, you might understand completely what is meant by the experience of physical life. The purpose of taking on physical flesh is, indeed, to experience physical life. As you do so, you are given the opportunity to enhance the ever-lasting emotion of love, and to overcome the weaknesses within yourself that are the end result of the original sin of separation, which was the separation of souls from God.

The soul, once given free will and free choice, left the comfort, safety, and sanctuary of the God-head and went out through the universes to experience for itself independent life, independent search for knowledge, and the sensation of physical experiences. You might consider this "the downfall" or "temptation." The soul became confused and lost its way as it took on the various vibrations, experiences, textures, and manifestations of material objects. You may think of this as the high, pure vibration of your soul becoming tarnished. It fell from piety and perfection into something less than perfect. From these depths, the soul became alone and was in despair. And from this point, the soul attempted to find its way back to God. It invoked the Law of Grace and repented. In short, it asked for help. There was a consideration or intervention from the God-head, and a way back towards perfection was established. Since that time, your soul has followed this course, meeting all things that it had met before, so that you might gain the knowledge of physical life and come to the greater understanding that you want to unite again in heaven and with God.

### Unconditional Love

From that perspective, taking on life in physical form as a human being can be considered as the expression of emotion. Emotions are of this dimension alone, and hence are temporal. Love is the only exception. Love is the only emotion that transcends the physical world. It is the only emotion that advances into the higher realms of the spiritual aspects. It is the purest form of God. Therefore touching upon pure love - love that comes without conditions or consequences, love that is always forgiving (in other words, unconditional love) - is what each of us attempts to do as we experience physical life. And as we touch upon unconditional love in ourselves, our souls might ascend to a higher level.

The physical world is a world of duality or extremes: light and dark, good and bad. The objective of your soul as it migrates through the physical world and physical life is to find a way to progress, in a balanced way between these extremes. This means putting limits on desires; finding a way to be temporal; and being tolerant of all things. Your attitude and reaction to physical events either move your soul forward (or progress), prevent your soul from moving at all (or to stagnate), or move your soul backward (or regress). Consequently, most souls struggle forward and backward as they attempt to move through the different levels of human experience: self awareness, self realization, full realization. Being fully realized is the highest level: to be conscious of yourself as a spiritual being while in the physical flesh. Those who make it to this level are considered saints or avatars: God in the flesh.

### Balance Between Extremes

A soul has no gender, yet it is a combination of both male and female aspects. The spiritual aspects of male and female are opposing aspects of the soul. If your soul were to enter the flesh consistently as one type of gender – for example the male – there would be an imbalance. You could live a consistent amount of lives in this way, developing the male gender to its greatest outcome or degree. However, for the balance of your soul, it must take on the opposite in gender so that both the female and the male physical aspects would be experienced. The intention, of course, is to move towards a position in which male and female would be balanced in both the physical aspects *and* the spiritual aspects. For example, the mannish man would become more gentle and lose his mannishness, simply becoming male in gender, and demonstrating the finer aspects - or the balanced aspects between male and female. Over the course of several lifetimes, the two extremes of gender are brought into a balanced form, both on a physical level and a spiritual level.

### *Karma – A Debt Owed to Yourself*

As your soul moves forward in a process of "self meeting self" in different experiences, things that are carried out in the physical world (and your attitude and reaction to them) either build up what you need to meet in another experience, or tear down what you have already taken to an extreme previously. This is the Law of Karma. It is in place in order to provide your soul with balance, for karma is a debt owed only to yourself, not to anyone else (as may be believed). The circumstances or conditions that you must meet in physical life are owed only to yourself. They exist for the single purpose of your advancement. They are to challenge you and are for you (and you alone) to meet. This form of action – this form of karma - exists to get you back on track to come to that point in which you can become individual, yet immersed in the God-head itself. Like an individual drop of water in the ocean, your soul is of itself, individual, but is part of the whole. This is what is meant by the phrase, "I am in my father, my father is in me." It is a consciousness individual, yet a consciousness of all, or the whole.

You have taken on physical life to make pefect yourself, your consciousness, your thinking and your beliefs. In your current life, your soul is, once again, attempting to touch upon pure love and become love complete. Difficulties, challenges or problems in life are actually stepping-stones to success or advancement, so how you view them determines your soul's progression. The demonstration of emotion is the key here. A good rule of thumb would be: What you see in others and you like or dislike - *to the same degree of emotion that you like or dislike them* - you like or dislike in yourself. If this quality was not within yourself, you would not be able to recognize it. Therein lies a way to gauge whether you are on track: looking at what is within yourself and what you like or dislike about yourself.

Picture an archer aiming an arrow at a target. The arrow is shot but it strays from the bull's eye. The object of karma is to get you back on track, back on that line between the commencement point and hitting the target dead center. Sickness, disease and illness tend to be the results of off-the-mark thinking. Conversely, difficulty and despair tend to be tools to put you back on track or back in line. For is it not only in the darkest hour, when times look their worst, that you would call out *"Dear Lord please save me?"* In a way, this is why all problems, challenges or difficulties come about: so you would come to that point (some would call it despair, others would call it realization) where you would need some assistance from God and the unseen world. For therein lies the point of perfection. You would be aided, assisted, forgiven, and consoled and you would advance forward out of this off-the-mark position and re-enter on the line towards the progression to perfection. In short, repenting or regretting pays off your karmic debt.

As you continue to move forward and attempt to be on the

straight and narrow path, your soul advances quickly. Rewards, abundance, or material wealth are given to you when you are in accord with truth and with being in balance with the spiritual laws (as well as manmade laws). When this is done, you might be considered as having "good karma,"or blessings. But, in fact, it is merely someone who is in balance and harmony with all things, trying to do good, willfully trying to be better, and earnestly attempting to overcome temptation.

### *Exercising Your Will Over Others*

Therefore, it is a function of reincarnation that as you advance in one life, you can advance further in the next, and the next. If you try with great earnest, you can return to the God-head in few life-times. Those who struggle and fall prey to temptation find their stay in the physical world to be extended, for they are building up in one experience what they must meet in the next one. A tyrant in one life will become a saint in another, in order to balance out these extremes. Someone who is evil, committing the most heinous crimes, must compensate by becoming the most saintly and productive person, doing good works in another life. Those who live by the sword, indeed die by the sword - either by their own hand or by that of another. Those who do good works and attempt to make the world and those in it better, reap great rewards of peace and tranquility and they are not alone in their old age. Those who find the way between living in the physical world, engaging in all its physical laws and yet who still attempt to live a balanced and productive life, finding out the spiritual laws, are those who advance the quickest.

You must go through physical life not in a state of worry or fear, and not using brute force to gain your will. It is easy for those who possess power or strength to use their force to inflict their will on others. As such, they sin. They are off the mark. For example, the prejudiced individual will come back as a member of the group which he or she had oppressed. A black man who is prejudiced against whites, for example, will come back as a white man who will befriend the black race. Likewise, the slave owner who whips and torments his slaves in one life would become a slave in another life-time, and be tormented to the same degree and the same extent as he had tormented others before. Each must understand what they give forth is retuned unto them, exactly. Not one iota more or less. Those who use their beauty or strength for great works continue to have blessings of great beauty or strength again and again. But those who *abuse* their beauty or strength may find themselves less than beautiful or strong in another life-time. For abuse of anything is considered "off the mark." As such, someone who commits such abuses must learn the lesson that what they had, they will have not - until they appreciate what they had. If they fail to understand their situation or circumstance, they are doomed to repeat the lesson again and again.

### Learning From Mistakes

Therefore, in the law of karma, and by the law of grace, you can advance to great heights by first deciding to do so. Secondly, you must willfully allow yourself to go through all the trials and tribulations of physical life, without malice, attempting to meet those things that are put in your path. To do so is to do your duty and to take responsibility with gladness and determination to overcome any trial or tribulation that comes your way.

Can you make mistakes, or must you suffer for all that you do?

Indeed you can make mistakes. King David was God's most blessed prophet because he made every mistake in the book *only once*. This means that there are ways to overcome the lessons of life. If you commit an error or make a mistake, and you learn by it, then there is no karma and, therefore, no need to re-experience the lesson. If you know better and you do something improper anyway, then you are off the mark, building that karma, for you have committed a sin, and you must pay for that transgression. For the bully in one life will be meek and bullied in another. But those who have great strength - and have the strength not to use it - are, indeed, blessed. With reason, tolerance, and acceptance, your soul can move forward. Reason allows you to prevent yourself from intruding or interfering in the life of another. If you *interfere* in another person's life, his or her problem (or karma) becomes yours. If you *intervene* in another person's life, however - shortening the outcome of what he or she is going through - you assist that person in meeting what he or she must meet. You do not detract from his or her path, nor do something for him or her. Rather, you assist him or her to advance and there is no attachment or karma for yourself. Therefore, always ask yourself if you are stealing the free will and free choice of another, for to do so is a cardinal sin.

### Live in the World

To comprehend reincarnation is to understand that you should always do things as if God were watching you. Ask yourself, "Would God like me to do this?" If the answer is no, then avoid it. If the answer is yes, then do it. Do not allow fear and worry to hold you back from the fullness of physical life. Be in the world and do not hide out from it. Those who lock themselves away from physical temptations of the material world are delaying their spiritual progress. Monasteries and sanctuaries are full of people who have turned their backs on the world but who have not met the temptations within themselves. Therefore, with the understanding of reincarnation, fully experience everything that the world has to offer, so that there is no temptation. Temptation left undone turns into great desires, and great desires turn into devious activity. Devious activities take you further away from the light or the path to the God-head.

Therefore, put limits on your desires - but do meet them. Be in the world, but do not be swallowed up by the temptations of physical life. For physical life itself is, indeed, a temporal thing. A rich man in one life-time may be a pauper in another. A thief in one life-time may be a police officer or judge in another. A soldier in one life-time may be a politician in the next. Your child in this life-time may become your parent in the next. These are examples of the checks and balances that exist so that you experience all aspects of physical life in a particular way. As one extreme is met in one life-time, it would be met by an equal and opposite extreme in the next (or, on occasion, in the same life-time).

### The Soul's Choice

However, pre-determined conditions of the physical world offer only lessons or opportunities for your soul. Understand that those who enter the world *have chosen to do so*. You chose the physical body you inhabit, the family in which you entered, the family's environment or location, and also the province, nation or region in which you were born. For in the pre-existence, the soul looks forward in time and "sizes up" the physical vehicle it is about to enter. Although the physical body never completely meets or *exactly* fits the needs of the soul, perfection is not necessary. Six to eight months prior to entering into the physical body, the soul determines all these criteria. If things change, the soul may vacate the physical body and go elsewhere to experience what it has chosen to experience, and another soul may "hover" over the potential mother, waiting for the moment to enter into the physical body.

It is your soul that chooses the body and the environment in which it is going to enter to experience physical life. There are no accidents or chances. The soul takes on a physical body that does not quite fit itself perfectly, but which will do. In doing so, the soul also absorbs or takes on some of the karma of the parents and the family. Therefore, entering into a physical body is extremely complex, but the soul has its ways and has those influences about it that would allow it to take on a physical body without much chance. Because the pattern of the body, the environment, the up-bringing, and the events in life are foreseen, there is a certain guarantee that the soul will be able to enter into a particular body to meet those things that it would be willing to meet (or must meet) for its own advancement and for its own purposes. Reincarnation, therefore, is not a haphazard thing. It is a willful progression of the soul selecting bodies, times, places, parents, families and circumstances that would suit it.

### Remembering Previous Lives

The soul does remember its previous experiences. In the first year of life, more so than the second or third year, the conscious mind retains these memories too. The tendencies, talents and abilities brought forth from previous experiences accompany the soul. When these particular aptitudes are demonstrated in a child, one might say the child is "a natural" or "it's in his genes." However, it might be better understood that the soul has a memory of those things that it has experienced in the past. It brings these natural abilities and tendencies into the present life from the past - as it does with all of its memories and its knowledge of the purpose for its present life. Indeed, you can meet those people in your present life who you have met in previous experiences, whether friend or foe, lover or enemy, parent or sibling. Certain feelings or sensations are brought forth and recalled in the present life based on experiences in previous life-times. Many people experience a sense of "déjà vu" or the feeling that they have met before, upon meeting some stranger. This feeling is not imagined, but is in recognition that you have had previous experiences with the person you believe you have just met.

### *Reincarnation in Other Species*

Animals, insects, plants - even microbes - have their own level of consciousness. Unlike humans, however, theirs are levels of consciousness without the ever-seeking internal aspect of the soul or the spirit, which is the force that motivates each and all of us to improve ourselves. Animals do reincarnate, however, and their consciousness changes species. A buffalo may become a deer, a leopard may become a rabbit, a mouse may become an elephant. Plants, being eaten by animals, take on a higher vibration, and in this respect their consciousness is moved forward or advances. They progress through these levels of consciousness so that they might come to a greater understanding or greater consciousness. While animals can develop and do change species, they do not interchange with humans, as they do not possess the consciousness of the soul mind or contemplative mind. For the soul mind is of a higher level or vibration than the greater consciousness in the animal, plant or mineral worlds. They do progress, however, and they do expand and become part of the greater consciousness, as all knowledge is of God and from God. But one does not enter physical life as a mosquito and exit it as an avatar.

### Remembering Your Past Lives

You can learn to discover your past lives by seeking through the records of your own mind and examining the record of previous existences through meditation. When you do this, you clearly see yourself in a previous life. This does take some effort and discipline to do, but those who have the ability, aptitude and desire to meditate and look introspectively may find these lives revealed to them.

Another way is to take stock of what you enjoy or detest. For instance, a young boy who picks up an old army bayonet and is fascinated with the short sword may be demonstrating that in a past life he was a soldier who used the sword. For the sword is more than simply a passing fancy: it is meaningful to him. When you read books or watch movies and consistently find yourself fascinated with, or siding with certain individuals or certain groups of people, this indicates that you have some attachment to these people. The key is in the level of emotion you experience. An Arabian Knight riding across the sand, waving a sword overhead excites some people. Those who proudly rode such a horse and waved the sword would be possibly remembering such existence. Those who are fearful of this scene, however, and are frightened by (or even deplore) sharp metal implements may be recalling a previous life-time when they were put to the sword. By taking a little stock in the things that you are absolutely fascinated by and the things that you absolutely deplore - without any real attachment or reason in your current physical life - you may reveal the innate memory of previous existences.

There is yet another technique to discern past lives. Look upon the face of another in low light. Do this by concentrating, but without focusing your eyes. The face of previous existences may come upon the face of that person you are viewing. For recorded on the face are all the life-times, one after the other. Whether a burly ruffian with long beard and bushy hair; or smooth, dark-skinned African; or small, dark-faced Aborigine; or glamorous aristocrat, noble ruler or humble stable-hand, old and young, male and female, the faces will appear. Simply gaze into or upon the face of another in low light and without focus of the eyes. You will see the record of the life-times that the other wishes to show.

However, examining a dream or vision in a state of meditation is a good way to recall who and what you were. There are, of course, mediation techniques that are guided or spontaneous to assist the recall of past lives. But in your dreams or visions you can also see past-life experiences *which now relate* to your present circumstances. In this way you are being given some knowledge, urging or suggestion from the contemplative mind as to how to handle a difficulty, challenge or pressure you are currently facing.

### Using Knowledge of Past Lives

Comprehension of your past life-times can help you to understand and cope with circumstances in your current life: your status, conditions, challenges or privileges. We have all heard of people born with physical deformities who grow up believing that God has cursed them. And we have all met people who face some great problem in life, and feel they do not deserve it. From a limited perspective, this does seem the case. But from the limitless perspective of the soul, it is not, for souls choose the circumstances in physical life that they want to experience. In the above examples, the soul has foreseen that it was going to be lame or maimed, to some degree. Its challenge in this physical life is to overcome this impairment by going through life in such a challenged way that may be helpful to others. By so doing, and living with such challenges, your soul will surge a little, and advance greatly.

If you understand that your soul has chosen to engage this particular challenge in your present life, then you can appreciate that this physical life is just one segment of the overall experience of your soul. Your soul, therefore, must *need* this difficulty. This, therefore, allows your mind to accept the challenge and to make the most of your life and your circumstances. One who is born into a position of privilege or greatness may feel undeserving and may suffer from feelings of great guilt. But that person has been given the greatest temptation: to over-indulge in all things. Perhaps he or she has entered into this life of privilege as a reward. Or perhaps the current circumstances have been set in place to test adherence to spiritual beliefs: will he or she resist the temptation to indulge in all of life's pleasures and live a life of hedonism, or will he or she choose to live a life of responsibility, using wealth responsibly so that others may prosper?

Now having said that, this does not mean you should give away all your money. As the saying goes, if you feed a starving man a fish, a blessing is owed to you. If you keep giving the man fish, and you exhaust your own resources, then you will both starve. But if you teach the man to fish, so that he might become independent and gather his own fish, you have not only saved yourself and your own resources, but you have made another person independent. Thus he is able to sustain himself and to give fish to others who might be in need. Figuring out how to do these things is, indeed, the proper application of life.

### *Summary*

If you wish to discover your own past lives, start off by looking at your tendencies. What is easy for you, and what is hard? Next, allow yourself to meet those things that you must meet to improve or advance your soul. Consider this example of two women faced with the same challenge in life. The first woman aspires to be a great dancer, but she loses the lower half of her leg in a car accident. The second woman also aspires to be a great dancer, and she, too, loses a leg. The first woman ends up living her life in self-pity, eventually becoming an alcoholic, embittered that her dance career is over. The second woman, however, endeavors to wear a prosthetic leg in order to see if she can dance again. She becomes determined to be the best one-legged dancer in the world, and because of this she achieves great fame and stardom. Her original goal of becoming a great dancer has been reached and she lives a happy, fulfilled life.

Which of these two women has correctly applied the rule of meeting what is given to you? Which woman faced herself and overcame her challenge? Obviously, the second one. Simply losing a limb was not going to deter her from attaining her goal. She already possessed the talent, but she just needed to find a different way to express it. All she had to do was look back in the past and find that she had great talent and ability. Therein lies the great understanding of having knowledge of previous life-times - knowing that you can meet what you are given in this life-time.

From a certain perspective, you may accept that the privileges that have come to you seemingly without effort are the result of the help you have given to other people in previous life-times. Maybe you helped others escape the executioner's chopping block, or perhaps you helped the poor and needy. In this life-time, therefore, you are being given assistance, as you have given assistance in the past. Each who seeks to understand his or her own life can come to some resolve as to why certain circumstances are now taking place. Knowledge of past life-times helps you to go through your present life. First, it may offer you an understanding of your predicament, and second, it may suggest how you might make something out of it – how to advance and overcome any inadequacy you are feeling.

If you would understand that this life is but one breath in the life of the soul, and that your soul experiences many, many life-times, then you would realize that you need not hurry through this life. You would take life and experience fully *all* that God and your soul have chosen for you experience. For to understand the past is to understand the future. Your future is built upon the experiences of the past. Now, this does not necessarily mean that just because you may have been an executioner in one life-time, you have to be one in your present one. It simply means that this is something you have done. What makes the difference is your attitude and understanding. Were you mean, vicious and cruel, maiming and torturing people, or did you take the executioner's job out of benevolence to relieve the suffering of those being beheaded? One choice is a sin and the other is a blessing.

Some people may experience very difficult times in their lives and they may have to do difficult things. Ask yourself, "Is this something God would like me to do? Would God approve of me doing this? Does this advance my soul?" Showing your willingness to do difficult things, and to remain unbiased, neutral or without emotion is the best that you can do in your situation of "self meeting self" - doing those things that you must do to advance your soul. It is not wrong to have pleasure or experience glad tidings, but it is wrong to willfully harm anyone else for your own pleasure, or to force your will upon someone else. Do those things that must be done practically and proficiently. Do those things without malice and meet those things without delay. Then you will have a fairly good grasp on how to meet all aspects of life without worrying about what is right or wrong and what might happen in the future. Address the issues at hand in the ever-present time and moment and attempt to do the best that you can do *with the knowledge you have.* If, in the future, you learn that something different could have been done, then add it to your knowledge and change your behavior. Do not drag yourself down into self-pity with feelings of guilt or remorse. Pick yourself up and be willing to meet all the difficulties of physical life. For it is only through meeting these difficulties that you move forward to the ever-present moment of unity and love. Life is a struggle. Learn to enjoy the struggle and learn to take time out to enjoy the passage of this life. For all too soon the candle will be extinguished and your life will be over. At the end of life, looking back, can you see accomplishments or not?

### One Soul, Many Lives
If you have grasped the concept of soul progression as a physical,

chronological advancement, here is another way to think of reincarnation. Picture a series of books side by side on a shelf. Each book represents one book of life. As you read through them from one volume to the next, you can see a progression from the beginning to the middle to the end - lives taking place in a linear or sequential way. But do not all the books on the shelf exist at the same time?

This is a difficult concept for our finite minds to understand – that all life-times exist at the same time, each going on as if you were reading a page in one book simultaneously with a page in the next book, and the next. In the ever-present moment, however each life already has existed and has been completed. All lifetimes, all experiences, all knowledge is now existing in this, the ever-present and everlasting moment. Comprehending this is to begin to understand the perspective of your immortal soul and the infinite consciousness of God.

# Chapter Six

# SPIRITUAL LAWS

## *Unconditional Love*

Many who seek enlightenment have pondered the question, "Do universal spiritual laws actually exist?" Indeed, such consistencies (or laws) governing your spiritual sojourn do exist. They are applied equally to all souls who have come to live in the physical world. All things are governed by the application and realization of unconditional love: love which is all-encompassing, all-surrounding and ever-present. Unconditional love, or love in its purest form, is the greatest law above all things, for love is of God and from God. In fact, love can be equated with God. It is like the rain that falls, or the sun that shines; for it touches on all: the good and bad alike. It is the type of love that loves all people, including those who have committed the most heinous crimes. For in essence, everything has its purpose, even though the purposes may confound, confuse, and contradict the finite human mind. However, the framework of unrestricted and unconditional love is for the advancement of the soul. Learning to apply unconditional love is the purpose of physical life itself.

## Law of Grace

The law of grace is the next greatest law, for it is an application of forgiveness, encompassing regret, repentance, and review of sinful acts, transgressions or intrusions. These aspects allow you (or more exactly, your high self, or soul mind) to find your way onto the proper path. When there is a recognition that you have not only erred, but that you have gone astray and are continuing to give into the negative aspects of your ego (i.e. temptation, self-gratification or self-aggrandizement), then difficulties occur in your life. Experiencing these difficulties should cause your soul - that force inside you that causes you to do right over wrong - to determine, through its own value, what is preferred and what is to be rejected. Then it knows to follow through with proper behavior. This allows forgiveness to enter into your life, so you no longer need to be punished or find yourself going through despair, difficulty, or some form of pain.

Therefore the law of grace can be summed up as a process of forgiving yourself and becoming able to overcome hardship, difficulty or pain in life. This law can be considered a realization within of some spiritual progression, advancement, or awareness to a higher level and proper thinking, believing and behaving. The law of grace, therefore, allows the intervention of angels, spirit guides, spiritual masters, teachers, and the more benevolent, advanced or evolved souls to come into your life and relieve your long-suffering. The law of grace is an action to forgive and remove difficulty or hardship from your soul while going through physical experiences. This can bring you relief, comfort, peace, affluence or material wealth. It can allow you a sort of free choice to avoid difficulty and aspire to great heights of prosperity or enlightenment.

## Law of Karma

As much as the law of grace allows you to avoid difficulty, hardship, poverty, isolation, desolation, and destruction, the law of karma allows things to be given to you that you deserve (and not one iota more or less). Those who initially approach this concept believe that karma is something that is owed from one person to another. To some degree this is true, but a more accurate understanding of the law of karma is that karma is something you owe yourself. In essence, karmic debt is a debt that you have incurred previously (in this life or in another) that you must pay back to yourself. However, for those who are new to this concept, it is acceptable to understand karmic debt as something that is owed to another. During one experience, some event occurred in which you made a transgression against another. To repay this transgression in your present life, either the other person is allowed to make a transgression against you, or you must do some favor or give some benefit to make up for your transgression. In this way, the debt is paid, the karma is met, the two are equal, and you can both move on. It is not necessarily that simple, however. Depending on the circumstances, a transgression you make against one person can come back to you from someone else. It is not necessarily the case that karmic debts are incurred from and repaid to the same people. This is why it is better to see karmic debt as a debt that is owed to yourself, or something which you are attempting to overcome. Again, this is a process of "self meeting self," or owing to yourself something you have previously spent.

It becomes evident, then, that there is a purpose, an ideal or a higher learning to take place. If someone eventually goes through enough experiences, learning what is the proper value or what is the proper reaction to take, then a time can come during which your soul becomes "debt-free" or more evolved. This greater level of awareness becomes self-awareness, which ultimately leads to self-recognition, self-realization and the highest level of human experience while in the flesh: full self-realization. This is the path of soul progression which all should aspire to.

As you become aware of your karmic debt, do not be afraid to take action or to react to others, for fear only limits your spiritual growth. Those who claim they do not want to make any mistakes (or who are afraid of making mistakes) are really admitting they are afraid to learn. Being willing to make mistakes is a demonstration of the willingness to learn, for you must always make mistakes when you learn. However, as you learn to forgive yourself or realize that mistakes and errors are essentially innocent, then you can make mistakes without incurring any karmic debt (and, therefore, the necessity to go through another experience to find out what went wrong). Why was King David God's most blessed prophet? Because he made every mistake – but only once. Do not be afraid to make mistakes, but do learn from them and endeavor not to repeat them.

In essence, karma can be likened to a two-sided coin. What is done on one side of the coin is done exactly on the other. There are, however, certain exceptions, for karma is given out exactly: not one iota more or less. You can, indeed, build a repertoire of karma, both good and bad. A simple way of understanding this is that good karma means rewards or blessings that come to you, whereas bad karma refers to difficulties, punishments or losses that come to you. Karma is given out at the appropriate karmic time, when you need it.

As you become aware that you are willfully supposed to go

through various experiences as part of your destiny (or life pattern), then you may begin to discern between those things in life that you *must do* out of necessity (which you cannot escape) and those things that you may *want to do*. When you determine this, and recognize that you have certain duties to perform, you perform your duties readily, aggressively and quickly, knowing that no one else can do your duties for you. If you have someone else do those things that are difficult, or which you are afraid or unwilling to do, then you not only cheat yourself of the experience, but you become destined to repeat the experience again. Think of these experiences as opportunities for learning. If you find yourself in the same circumstances over and over again, you are, perhaps, failing to perform a certain duty or make a particular choice in life. Those things one may wish to do some day, on the other hand, may or may not get done immediately. Discerning between the two allows you a clear understanding of what to do and what not to do.

Free will and free choice are the greatest gifts of all. They were given to souls prior to the original sin - the sin of separation of souls from God. Using the mechanism of free will and free choice, they chose to advance themselves, some choosing to become ingrained in matter and material, physical things. As they did so, they became dense and darkened. However, as those souls learned to overcome the temptations of the flesh or the material world, they began to ascend or advance themselves to the level of greater consciousness. This ascension is done by accepting duty and rushing to do it without hesitation.

How you react to any given circumstance determines the karmic response or how karmic debt is built. Generally speaking, what you do out of necessity or duty does not hold much in the way of baggage or karmic debt. This is not the case if there is some emotion that is involved. Consider the following example regarding the taking of another's life. As part of his purpose in life, a young man becomes a soldier, and in order to protect his people, he is required to kill another. This taking of life may be seen as negative karma, which would be repaid in kind by the fallen soldier in some future life-time. It need not be, however, such that this karmic wheel would spin endlessly: one person killing another one time, only to have this same experience done to him or her in the next one. Instead, the attitude of the first soldier should be one of duty, without remorse, joy, hatred, condemnation, glee or exultation. It should be done merely as one soldier meeting another with one soldier being eliminated, and the other moving on.

This is the way to proceed in all circumstances: doing your duty without any emotional attachment. Emotions tend to build up karmic reaction, necessitating the revisiting or re-experiencing of the same circumstances. This sometimes happens during the same lifetime, or may happen in another life-time, for karma is continual until it has been met or finished. How do you know it is met or finished? Examine yourself when an event is completed. Do you feel anxious, frustrated, angry, or resentful? Are you filled with a sense of hunger for more, or do you experience regret or revisiting of the situation over and over in your mind? When a karmic debt has, indeed, been balanced, there is no emotional response whatsoever. A certain sense of neutrality or peace comes over you. In most circumstances, you can use this to monitor whether or not your duty has been done and you are free to move on from any form of harm or transgression against any other.

Once you discern what is your duty, get busy and get it done. Do the best you can, always looking for improvement or advancement or a better way to handle a circumstance or situation. Do not allow yourself to become triggered into some arbitrary, immediate and poorly thought-out response, for this is more on the animal or emotional level. Like an animal that is bitten on the leg, you can choose to react similarly by biting back immediately, without any reflection. But those who aspire to a higher level of consciousness learn not to react in the same manner in which they were provoked or harmed. Instead, they choose to react on the higher levels, and therefore they persist. Karma, therefore, is both a simple, yet complicated law, for it is distributed equally from one soul to all souls, back to the same soul again. As a rule of thumb, when there is a neutral feeling, when there is no reaction one way or another, then, to some degree, you can believe that your karmic debt has been met and you have come to a situation or position in which there is no karmic debt one way or the other. The reverse is true to advancement, prosperity, or privilege, however. Always doing good and looking out for others tends to build up a positive aspect of karma, which comes in handy when you need a favor (so to speak) from that which is slightly beyond your consciousness.

### Free Will and Free Choice

To recognize whether or not you are advancing, first of all understand that you possess your own free will and free choice. This particular law has been in place since the beginning. As you advance through life, realize that everyone rests on his or her own responsibility. When you take responsibility for yourself, then you will not sit still, complain or procrastinate. Instead, you will take action, get things done and move forward, taking responsibility for your own actions. This allows you to aspire to the greater level of consciousness. It also allows you to become more aware of the interaction of each soul mind with each other. This, then, allows you to do a self-evaluation. This self-evaluation is from the greater consciousness, for on the animal level, the response is emotional: either flee or fight. An animal retaliates with all things. You can overcome these immediate tendencies or Neanderthal reactions with your higher mind, sophistication, or evolution. The situation becomes controlled and you prevent yourself from going outside of this point of reference. You remain peaceful, and you do not allow the emotions to trigger a reaction to any given thing. The function of this is such that you can recognize within yourself the higher good, the higher value. Recognize that when you see something in another as either good or bad, you are recognizing this as being part of yourself, for if it were not part of yourself, you would not recognize it. For instance, you may observe, "Gee that person always likes to put people under her thumb," not realizing, of course, that you like to do this yourself. To the same degree of emotion as you recognize, feel or sense this observation, you are guilty of exhibiting it yourself. In recognizing what you perceive outside of yourself, you recognize it because it is within yourself. This, therefore, allows you to recognize areas of improvement within yourself. Recognizing that someone is conceited may be one indication of a conceit within you - to the same emotional experience or expression.

### Standing Up to the Strong When they are in the Wrong

Another spiritual rule is to stand up to the strong when they are in the wrong. The other aspect of this particular law is to make concessions for the weak or the meek. It concerns taking action and avoiding karmic debt at the same time. Indeed, standing up to the strong when they are in the wrong allows you to decide if you will stand up to transgressors. The sin of omission or complacency is just as strong a sin as that of commission, you see. This, therefore, allows you to properly apply your God-given skills, talents and abilities to combat, object to, or reject any thing, knowing you are fully righteous in doing so, while at the same time, leaving room for avoiding mishandling the weak or the infirm. By standing up to the strong when they are in the wrong, - while making concessions for the weak - you do a great service to yourself, which indeed adds a blessing. Justice is the great equalizer in the universe, for it allows peace into the hearts of all. To be just or to stand up for justice's sake is indeed a righteous thing to do. It not only allows you to always take the high road, but also to experience those things that you have brought into the world previously. In attempting to experience these things again, there is a certain level of peace, tranquility, and recognition of proper action and inaction.

### Other Laws

In conjunction with justice, there is a certain law of recognition, which is that you should only repeat things you know for sure, not rumor or hearsay (and nor should you provoke the same). If you were to see someone getting into a green car, for instance, all you could say is, "I saw someone getting into a green car." To imply without direct observation or knowledge that the person is stealing the car, sabotaging it, or is about to take parts from it is sinful, and, as such, you would become subject to a loss of karma. Be cautious in your judgment, as this tends to prevent you from making mistakes or jumping to irrational conclusions. Understand that there is a great equalizer. The karmic effect is such that your appearance in the world at certain times, in certain environments is a demonstration of your free will and free choice. A soul chooses to enter into a particular body, within a particular mother, and within a particular family (not to mention the household, extended family members, the neighborhood, city, state, region and country of the world) to take on physical life. This allows your soul, or the karmic determination of your soul, to be able to select the life it is about to take on in advance. The soul makes all these considerations in the pre-existence.

For there is a particular law, such that a soul experiences different lifestyles in different places in the world, because it is proper to do so. One does not come back to the same part of the world over and over again. But in this choosing, it is the law that a soul is determining, and has itself to blame or praise for its advancement into a particular environment. It has its reasons for choosing to incarnate as it does, and in choosing the life it wishes to live. Those influences upon a soul would be emotional aspects of prejudice, abuse of authority, power, or the enjoyment of the soul over others, as well as the desire to be a recluse or loner, avoiding contact with people altogether.

There is another law of difficulty or physical ailments in the body. Difficulty in the stomach, for example, may indicate irritation from worry, fear, and other such adversely-influencing emotional aspects. Emotions are the constructive and destructive forces in any body, and they cause physical ailments to appear or not appear. The rule here is that you should be honored and that peace should reign supreme under all circumstances and conditions. When you have experienced a sufficient number of lives and know that you can handle whatever comes at you, regardless of what it is, only then can you come to a point of believing this. This law is a law of justice in a certain way. But this belief is built upon your experiences and knowledge that God, which is a loving and just God, would never give you more than what you can bear. But this is an act of faith. Keeping your peace and faith and not allowing yourself to be triggered into other contests, confrontations or distractions, indeed, is the blessing here that comes from the experience you are gathering in this life-time.

# Chapter Seven

# SPIRITUAL BEINGS: ANGELS, GUIDES AND GHOSTS

### *Discarnate Souls*

When the soul takes on the flesh and enters into a physical body, it is like a genie entering into a bottle. The soul is the essence of a person. It is the consciousness and sum totality of you. It is immortal. During the time after physical death, when the body (or the shell) is set aside, the part that was whole before it came into the physical body returns once again to its normal, immortal state. It returns to being a discarnate being. The soul, therefore, exists both within the flesh and without it. Leaving the body behind, it becomes a "free agent," having the ability to go to other dimensions, visit other worlds and ascend to higher levels of consciousness.

You can picture these levels as a hierarchy with ghosts at the bottom; then spirit guides and angels who are interested in certain individuals above that; then religious figures, saints and avatars who have the ability to assist or visit others when asked through prayer above that. Above is an even higher level of spiritual beings.

### Ghosts

In simple terms, a ghost is little more than a soul that is discarnate, or has set aside its body. Usually, however, a ghost is an entity who is earth-bound, stuck in an in-between world that some have termed the "astral plane." It is a soul that is not aware that it has made the transition from physical life to physical death and does not understand its new reality. This being, therefore, it appears to those who see it as a shadow of its former self, moving about in low light. It may appear smoky, milky-white, liquid or fluid. It is often called "ectoplasm." It may also appear as lights or colors, in the shape of a series of golden or sky-blue orbs. Or it may appear as a twinkling star or a light that twinkles on and off. It may also appear as two brackets held together in the shape of an orb or sphere. It may appear in any of these forms, but it is still the consciousness or the essence of a particular person. When you perceive a ghost, you are witnessing the soul in the different forms or shapes that it is able to take on. A ghost is little more than the appearance of a soul which is not inhabiting a physical body. It has the same usual personality traits as it had when it was in physical life.

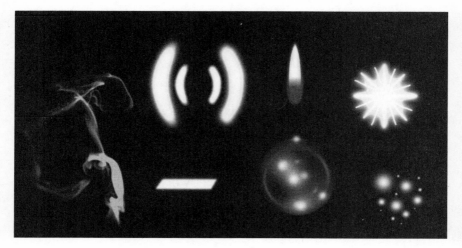

## *Angels and Spirit Guides*

An angel is a person who is discarnate, but who has an interest in the welfare of someone else here in the physical world. An angel has the ability to assist in the lives of people - he or she can talk to, visit, coach, or oversee them. Spirit guides (or guardian angels, or some may call them) are of this same high spiritual level or consciousness. Beings at this level are able to assist or intervene (but not necessarily to interfere) in the life of someone they are interested in. Therefore, they are able to guide with a few words, a phrase, or a demonstration. Like a ghost, they may appear in a vision while the person is awake or in a dream during sleep states. They appear differently than ghosts, however; not as a milky-white substance or light, but in a shimmering, translucent form (depending upon individual advancement or enlightenment).

Other spiritually-advanced beings - gurus, prophets, saints, or avatars - also have the ability to do this sort of apparition. However, they may do so while they are still here in the flesh. They appear translucent, as if in a kind of photograph, and can visit those individuals who they are overseeing or guiding through physical life - while living their own lives at the same time. These are highly-developed souls, indeed, who can visit others in this state. Unlike angels, they are visible in the physical world and participate in real time. As such, when a higher-developed being projects him or herself to wherever he or she wishes to be - the devotee, student, adept or some other party he or she is interested in helping — he or she may speak longer sentences and participate in longer discussions.

## *The Highest Level of Spiritual Being*

The next level of spiritual beings above this one includes religious figures who have gone to the highest spiritual level - such as Jesus Christ, Mohammed, Buddha, Moses, and Krishna - as well as angels who have never incarnated in the flesh - such as Reuben or Michael. These angels have an even greater purity of thought, being, and essence, as they have not been tempted or affected by the physical world (nor have they entered into carnal pleasures). From this level, they have a certain degree of pious attitude or ability. As they are closer to the God-head, their visits to the physical world tend to be rare. Together with the religious leaders and spiritual teachers, these are the highest level of angel: a sort of inner circle of the most developed souls. On the one hand are those who have not entered into the flesh and have arrived at such a high level, even though they have taken on the flesh. On the other are those who have not taken on a physical body, and have not taken on the karma and responsibility, (nor have they become caught up in the temptations of carnal sensation). Like a pillar, they represent two sides of the same experience. There are those who have advanced forward, overcoming all the temptations of the world, and who have risen to such a high spiritual level that they become examples, way-showers and teachers for others. From time to time, they may incarnate in the physical world again, in order to help those souls still malingering within the physical world to advance themselves. For the intention is for all souls in the world to arrive at the higher levels of consciousness: totally aware, totally self-aware and fully self-realized as a spiritual being, having overcome all the temptations of the physical world. In other words, an angel, an avatar, a God-like being. In essence, those who have gone on, and who lived life, willfully attempting to aspire to the highest level of consciousness and be an example to others, come back to teach others who are here now. They do not waste their knowledge and simply "retire" once they die. When they leave this physical dimension for the higher spiritual level, they become spiritual beings such as saints, avatars, and angels. They return to the physical world to share with their brothers and sisters what they have come to understand by overcoming the challenges of physical experiences and living as a physical body. And this is done selflessly, so that all can progress.

### *Sensing the Presence of a Spiritual Being*

When you are in the presence of a highly-developed being, there is an all-encompassing sense of well-being or love. However, when you are in the presence of a lower-developed spiritual being - those who are not of the finest vibration but are of the coarser or more mundane vibrations and those who are still ingrained in the heavy denseness of carnal experiences - you may feel dread. Understand that the spiritual world has different dimensions, like different rooms in the same mansion. Those who are living in the cellar are earth-bound and selfish in nature, whereas those who dwell on the higher floors are of a finer or greater vibration. Those who live on the lower levels seek only self-gratification and self-subsistence. They are the least intelligent and least in the way of concern for helping anyone (save for themselves). By contrast, those at the higher levels exist in an unselfish world, attempting to advance or lift up to the higher levels of consciousness all those who wish to. Therefore, these higher beings give off a sense of euphoria or well-being; a feeling of being surrounded by love, peace and protection. To those who are attracted to lower-end spiritual beings, there is a feeling of dread or despair, coolness, and a sense of pain. These poor, misguided souls have not fully realized how to advance to the higher levels of existence or consciousness. If you seek out the spiritual dimensions, you can usually avoid these lower entities by striving to ascend beyond the astral plane and beyond the levels of the mundane. You will experience a feeling of great uniformity, welcome, peace, relief, and (most importantly) a profound sense of unconditional love and belonging.

You may also feel the physical touch of a spiritual being. Sometimes it is felt as a cold hand on your shoulder. Sometimes it is felt as a prickle of electricity or energy dancing upon your body. Sometimes it is felt as if an invisible person is laying on top of you, or sitting beside you in bed, or holding your hand and gently squeezing it. In its immortality, the soul has a physical essence, and spiritual beings have a real physical quality. The soul takes up space and has a density that you may see, sense, or feel the touch of, if you are perceptive and open to the spiritual world.

Generally speaking, children are better able to perceive spiritual beings than adults. Children see without prejudice, and because of this, they naturally perceive things a little easier than adults can. For all of the life, the conscious mind of the adult is trained to selectively see, hear and feel things that it has been taught are real and not to witness or sense those things that it has been taught are unreal. Therefore children who have not had this natural ability taught out of them can see those things that are a little higher in vibration. Also, children do not have the prejudice or fears that can negate an adult's ability to experience communication from the spiritual dimensions. And children are a little closer to these dimensions, for they have only recently come into the physical world from the pre-existence themselves. As such, they still have some recognition, logical understanding, or memory of the beings that co-existed with them in the pre-existence. It is, therefore, easier for a child to see spiritual beings without the blindness or the spirit of forgetfulness which prevents many adults from perceiving them. And as such - sometimes very clearly and without difficulty - they carry on lengthy conversations with them. Remember that beings who are discarnate are not deceased. They are simply discarnate souls who wish to participate in this physical dimension with those to whom they hold some meaningful affection or purpose.

## *Your Spirit Guides*

Most of us have more than one guardian angel or spirit guide. In the pre-existence, each soul who strives to enter into the physical, corporeal world makes an agreement, deal or strategy with other souls who are willing to participate - from an observational point of view - in his or her experiences. You are surrounded by spiritual guides, or (more exactly) students who attempt to watch the process of your soul going through the physical trials and tribulations of the world. They have made agreements to assist you. They attempt to overcome the inadequacies and difficulties of your physical life. They also help to arrange all the necessary or suitable experiences so that your soul may experience all that it has entered into the world to do.

There are also other spiritual beings who are relief-intended. These angels answer the call when you enter a situation of great despair, and are in need of the law of grace to be applied. For God is so loving that God would have none suffer, save those who choose to do so. There is great wisdom and great knowledge that can be obtained from those who are beyond the physical world. You must be willing to listen, set aside your will, and pray for intervention in your life. There are those beings who accompany you throughout your life and there are even more powerful beings who are able to change the course of your life, as you come to understand what your soul is attempting to learn here. Once this occurs, there is no need to be redundant and continue to learn through hardship. You can move on to higher levels of learning. It may take a higher-developed mind or an angel of great power and resource to shift or change your spiritual path in life, but certainly there can be an intervention - always towards your welfare and advancement.

To understand how this works, imagine a grandparent over-seeing you. Then picture a group of your siblings who wish to go along with you and watch all your physical experiences at the same time. Along the way there may be bullies, and jealous or misguided people interfering in your life a little. They may need to be chased away, and this can be easily done. Those spiritual beings who are mischievous and who wish to interfere and cause difficulty in your life are of a lower vibration. You need not fear these minds at all, for they do not have authority to be in a physical body. Unless fear is given to them, you can drive them away rather easily. Fear empowers mischievous beings (or misguided souls) to have some dominance over you. A fast solution is to ask for a higher being to chase away the unwanted influences that are mischievous, detrimental and disturbing to you. Simply state, "Dear Lord: please protect me from any and all negative influences, regardless of source."

# CHAPTER SEVEN

## *Communication with Discarnate Souls*

Any and all who wish to communicate with angels, spirit guides or the souls of any who have passed from the physical world can do so through the records of their own minds (i.e. through meditation and dream states). If there is the desire, it can be done without the assistance of anyone else. But understand that no more authority should be given to any discarnate soul than to anyone else - or to yourself. You have the right to be in the physical world. You have a mission and a purpose that is paramount and important to yourself and to others. Those who are discarnate may not have the same sense of urgency or importance as you, and they certainly do not have the same right to be in the world as you do (otherwise, they would take on life and incarnate into another body of their own). Ask yourself why you wish to communicate with one who has passed on. While they are in the pre-existence or the dimension beyond the physical world, discarnate souls are not allowed to *interfere* in the life of anyone. They may only *intervene* when asked to do so.

During the states of sleep, your soul can leave your physical body temporarily and visit other souls who are discarnate in such dimensions. Due to your advancement (or level of understanding) in your mind, you have the ability to go to these places for counsel, reconciliation, or to go over some problem or concern. For instance, a child looking for guidance from his or her recently-deceased father would be given direct communication. The father would certainly wish to protect and inform his children, and his mind would reach down from above (so to speak), meeting the other mind reaching up from below. If there is the need, communication with a loved one after physical death is certainly possible.

### *Third-party Contact: Mediums and Clairvoyants*

You may also use a medium to contact discarnate souls, but mediumship should not be considered as any more than a way to contact those minds who have some desire or need to communicate with you. Mediumship tends to lead one into contacting souls who are in the lower realms, caught in the astral plane, or who are ingrained in the physical world. These souls are of the lower vibrations, and they thirst for even a brief breath in the world that a medium can provide them. On the other hand, those souls who are of the higher vibrations may speak through a medium or appear to someone who is clairvoyant, if they wish to intercede in the life of another. Of course, they may speak to the individual directly as well. They may appear to give some message or piece of advice to the person in whose life they are attempting to intervene. But unless there is some purpose, benefit, or construction to it, communication may not take place. If the experience is of little purpose or meaning (other than to prove there is an existence in the dimensions beyond), it is likely the experience would not take place at all. There needs to be a very important purpose or reason for this communication to take place. Not only does it require some energy or concern from the medium to be the facilitator between the physical and spiritual worlds, it takes a huge amount of energy for a discarnate soul to appear in the physical world.

As a rule of thumb, the communication must have some noble or meaningful purpose. Usually if there is a need, there will be a visit and some communication from a soul beyond the physical world. Keep in mind that the only difference in this particular circumstance between yourself and those souls who are in the spiritual world is simply that they have given up their physical bodies. For whatever reason, they no longer need the weight of the physical body, nor are they attached to the world, engaging in its temptations. There are, however, people who can communicate with souls who have passed on; for each and everyone of us possesses the ability to communicate with those souls with whom we have some meaningful connection or affection. Usually there is no such communication with those you hate or despise. But, out of love, those who would wish to communicate with you for some beneficial purpose can easily do so.

## Asking for Spiritual Guidance and Assistance

Asking for guidance or assistance from an angel, spirit guide or some other soul who has left the physical world can be done easily, as long as you do so without fear, excitement or any kind of emotion whatsoever. You should also approach this act with some degree of patience or acceptance, and there should be a purpose for it. Do you wish to communicate only to prove to yourself the existence of angels, spirit guides, or a friend or lover who has gone beyond? If this is the purpose, then it may not be a high priority in the minds of those who have gone beyond the physical world. So first have some meaningful purpose. Next, commit a prayer for protection, saying, "Dear Lord, please protect me from any and all negative influences, regardless of source." During meditation, reach high up with your mind and form a picture or ideal of what the spiritual being you wish to contact would look like. It is best to have no emotion or expectation one way or the other. Then, as if a veil were lifted, the spiritual being can easily communicate with you. But understand that with patience and with some sincere interest in this, these beings will gladly appear to you during your dream states as well. The real difficulty lies in the person who is in the physical world, rather than in those who look back on the place from whence they came. Therefore, try to be as calm as when you are asleep. But do have an idea or question to ask or some mission or purpose in mind. Any and all can communicate with those who have gone on before. Usually there is a bond of love, attachment or affection between the souls, and this makes the visitation more purposeful (and, therefore, easier to do).

After you commit the prayer, and seek out communication through meditation or dreams, then listen. As you commit your prayer, you will hear a voice from within: the still, small voice of your soul. You may also see your loved one in a dream or meditation. He or she will not speak in volumes of words. The communication will be short and concise, limited to a few words, a phrase, or perhaps a sentence. Mischievous or misguided souls, on the other hand, have great volumes of words as they attempt to influence you. At first, their comments may be sweet to the ear, but gradually they will turn provocative, profane and lewd. Those who practice with a pendulum, Ouija board, automatic writing or any other such go-between method of spiritual communication must be particularly concerned not to attract such lower minds, as they will fill up your communication with gobbledygook. Instead, speak to the higher spiritual realms. They will be benevolent and direct, and they will never misguide you or tell you what to do. Any spiritual entity that says to you that something in particular *must be done* is usually a deceiver. Seek out those who will suggest the correct answer or the correct way for the betterment of all. Do not fear them, but embrace them. You will be able to trust that what is given to you is meaningful.

But look upon the beginning time as a simple time of meditation. Spiritual beings should not be regarded as a source to be relied upon for daily information-gathering or guidance. It is a resource to be called upon in times of need. In the meantime, simply ask the unseen world for assistance to fulfill your destiny and meet your purpose in life. Indeed, spiritual beings may do those things that you would wish them to, but first you should pray and have your prayer be consistent with your actions and expectations. It is a complete waste of time to pray for those in the spiritual world to advance you a million dollars, for there is no money in the spiritual world. Those souls in the spiritual world have no interest in (or use for) money. They do, however, have an interest in your welfare and advancement. A much more valuable prayer (than to ask for money to be sent to you through some lottery, windfall or by magical manifestation) would be to ask for assistance in making you more prosperous. The other way does not usually work at all.

Your expectations, therefore, must be with some degree of understanding the nature of the spiritual world. Overcoming hardships in life, and the inadequacies and character flaws within you are usually for the further advancement of your spiritual aspects. The preferred way to use the spiritual aspects is to live your life filled with peace and prosperity so you may still overcome the inadequacies within, but in a benign and easy way.

### Overcome Your Fear of Evil Spirits

While there are no truly "evil" spirits, *per se*, misguided souls with evil tendencies towards self-satisfaction and self-gratification do exist. As you sojourn into the spiritual worlds, you should be aware of them, and be respectful and mindful of them. Understand that there are none, however, who are more powerful than you. Unless you are involved in the forces of darkness, dread, despair and self-destruction, you never have to venture into their "neighborhood" in the first place. Instead you rise up to a higher level of consciousness. When someone turns on the light or opens the door of a dark room, what happens to the darkness? Where does it go? It vanishes in the instant the light appears. It hides in all the nooks and crannies of the room. You are the light that illuminates the room, causing the darkness to flee. That light is the strength, power and understanding of any who are advancing themselves, who have tendencies to do good, and who allow the spirit within to make them adhere to those things that are for the greater good. It is that force within that always lead you to self- examination, so that you might advance - overcoming the inadequacies, difficulties, hardships, or rough edges of yourself - into a more finer, perfect, more enlightened being. Like light coming into the dark room, your soul chases away all the elemental beings (or so-called "evil influences") which are poor, misguided, and selfish in their tendencies. They cannot stand the light of day. The light of day is your soul illuminating the situation with love and understanding, and your ability to call upon even more souls from the higher spiritual dimensions to bring more light.

Therefore, do not fear the darkness. Do not fear those who are misguided - but do not encourage them either. Refrain from participating with them and from allowing your will to be controlled by any other (through such practices as automatic writing, pendulum swinging, or consulting a Ouija board). But go slowly. By going slowly, you avoid the unknown and uncertainty, which allows you to know what path to take. With familiar experiences or steps, you will not need to come in contact with what may be called "the forces of darkness," or those poor and misguided souls. Instead, you will be able to avoid them and ascend to the higher levels of consciousness. Always look higher, towards the light and to those minds who are illuminated and of a finer and higher vibration. Those who are stuck in the mire will sooner or later pull themselves out and follow in your footsteps to the higher realms. Avoid those with evil as their intention. Do not pay attention to them. Do not think of their existence at all - but be mindful that they do exist and that they may distract and torment you (or even cause disturbances in your life). But they are of no consequence. They have no power or right to be in the world, as you yourself do. No one needs to fear these small-minded, selfish, carnally-interested, misguided minds. Open the door. Let the light shine in the room and they will flee or vanish for their very existence. Look to the light. Look to life.

## Summary

Realize that you are not alone in the world. The essence of reaching out to the higher levels or consciousness (in which you would find those spiritual beings that would care for you) is to find yourself in a state of well-being, surrounded by love that is unconditional, non-judgmental, and non-prejudicial. These souls are your friends and relatives from previous experiences. They love and cherish you and would gladly assist you and conduct you through the higher dimensions to help you overcome the challenges of life. Indeed, your chosen angel would help relieve conditions of despair, loneliness, hurt and pain - as would others who have gone before and who understand your path and plight. There have been many, many humans who have transcended the difficulty of physical life and who have touched upon the highest possible consciousness and the highest possible existence in the human experience while they were alive in the flesh. They would gladly help their brothers and sisters to follow their footsteps and ascend to the greatest level of all: to touch upon the Christ Consciousness: that which is of God and from God; the inner essence of love that is supreme.

As you ascend, you will understand that everything in the spiritual world is but an extension of yourself - your state of mind, your understanding - and the experiences that you have had, or the level of enlightenment that you have achieved. Always aspire to the higher and greater forces of light and love. You will not be disappointed, nor will you be left alone. Pray for help. Pray for opportunity. Pray for those who would bring you opportunity - whether they are in physical form or not. You are never alone.

# Chapter Eight

# SPIRITUAL ABILITIES

Spiritual abilities (also referred to as spiritual gifts) are demonstrations of the creative essence of your soul. All that you witness in the flesh is a demonstration of this higher level of mind, this aspect of creation itself. For the nature of the mind is such that it can create positively or create negatively: it can make life, or it can destroy it. However, it is God's ultimate privilege, intent or aspect to be the creator or the destroyer, free of any influence, karma, or explanation. Humans are but a receptacle, the entire make-up of a thought or thought-form taking on flesh: a soul incarnate. As such, it is God-like, a pro-creator, for as it has often been said, mankind was made in God's own image. This is true when you look at humans at the soul level.

*The Creative Force*

The spiritual abilities that are demonstrated in various people are examples of the living soul within the temple, or the body. These include knowing in advance things that are yet to take place, or a simple awareness of those things yet to be. This can be demonstrated by the ability of premonition, precognition, prediction, and prophecy and would be accompanied by clairsentient ability, clairaudient ability and clairvoyant ability (i.e. clear feeling, clear sensing, and clear seeing). The ultimate demonstration of the creative force within, however, is the ability to bring life to another (i.e. to procreate). Procreation is the exemplification of building one physical body within another. While this is the ultimate in creativity, the reverse also holds true. Anyone can be "creatively destructive." You can damage anything. There may be a thousand ways for you to cause death to another, but can there be a thousand ways to bring life back? No. Only the creative force has that power. It can bring creative life back into the material world. This is the difference. Even a child can bring destruction to something, but it takes a great mind, indeed, to bring back even a simple life (or even to bring improvement in physical condition) to anything. This should be cherished.

The abilities to foresee, foretell, be aware of, or understand demonstrate the creative force of your soul mind (or contemplative mind) in line with your conscious mind. The recognition of this additional, extrasensory information comes from the willingness of your "low self" to accept guidance from your "high self."

### Dreams and Mind Projection

Dreams are an exemplification of what takes place during sleep states, when the mind reaches out. This is a projection of the mind, or the soul out of a physical body (also referred to as astral travel). It is the ability to visit higher levels or planes of learning or understanding, in order to bring back into the physical world some bit of information you need to add to the record of your soul. Like gathering ingredients for a certain recipe, your soul sojourns to higher planes for whatever it needs: a solution to some problem, an answer to a question, or some direction for action.

## *Dowsing*

There is also the ability to extend your senses through the human energy field or aura for dowsing, automatic writing, or other forms of information-gathering. When put into a state of deep relaxation, the body may be put "on hold" as if you were outside of yourself. You are able to take on information and bring it back for use in some practical application, such as using a dowsing rod to indicate a lost article. This is commonly used to locate precious metals, oil, gas and underground streams. Those who are more adept could use this to dowse out conditions of illness within a body. Again, these are demonstrations of what is already evident in you: your soul mind or contemplative mind. While these are the more simplistic ways of gathering information, they are also the more dangerous, however. For in giving up conscious control, you leave yourself open and vulnerable to potential influence and harm. Caution, therefore, must be exercised.

## *Inspiration*

There is also the ability to have great knowledge and to be inventive. This demonstrates the ability of tapping into certain levels of consciousness or learning and bringing back information. It may occur in an instant; such as someone who is intuitive contemplating a problem; or it may be someone who is visionary seeing a vision or having an outline in the mind's eye; or it may be a prophetic mind seeking information in a vision, dream, or state of meditation. All are demonstrations of this ability. This also includes people who have a "feeler type" of mind. They do not rely on their visionary skills to know whether something is right or wrong. They feel it. They experience a sensation of heat or cold in their solar plexus, shins, legs, palms, head or some other part of the body. All of these are demonstrations of the same ability.

### Practice Your Abilities

Some people practice their spiritual abilities more than others, and therefore they become better at expressing them. Understand this as a language: the language of the soul. Pictures and symbols are the language. Learning what the pictures mean allows you to become better suited or acquainted with your spiritual abilities. Telepathy and telekinesis are good examples of this. With practice, an individual may become much better as a telepath, sending or receiving thoughts (or sometimes both). They may even become better able to control physical matter (i.e. telekinesis). For example, a chiropractor with such ability can cause the bones to shift or change almost effortlessly during an adjustment. Largely it is a question of valuing your own abilities, as opposed to someone else's. But if there is a desire to develop your intuition, it is not a matter of learning it, but a matter of *recalling* it. It is a matter of getting yourself "out of the way," so to speak, by eliminating thoughts of disbelief, and the feelings of wonder and excitement that something "extra-special" or extraordinary is happening. If there can be a careless or non-emotional state during these times, then you may more fully experience communication at this level. Your intuition, therefore, would become more accurate. As in life, it is largely your emotional responses that prevent you from moving forward. Try to perpetuate an emotional state of detached optimism. Look for the ability, but be calm and unemotional. Don't let your own emotions get in your way.

## *The Soul is Cautious*

All examples of spiritual gifts and gathering extra information - from visiting other dimensions, to speaking with angels, to witnessing the shape and color of an aura - are only what you already understand, know, and have used in previous experiences or life-times. Learning to forgive others, learning not to be judgmental, and learning not to be necessarily right all the time are precursors to the demonstration or advancement of these abilities in you. A soul is quite a cautious thing. As each soul advances in its own personal sojourn to touch upon the face of God, once again, and become enveloped in the ever-present moment and sense of great love, it advances quietly and slowly. In this regard, when you touch upon the face of God, or you communicate with your high self, you become a creator in a positive sense, and you bring more light into the world. In essence, if what you gather is not helpful, or if it does not perform some service or purpose and is merely entertaining (such as bending a spoon or wishing something into being), it is useless. It is the application of how each of us relates to one other that is important. In this way, it is a demonstration of tolerance and acceptance, and thus, brings us closer to God

# Chapter Nine

# MEDITATION

Meditation is a mental practice in which the ordinary thoughts of the day and the rational mind are put to rest, brought under control, or brought into a state of discipline so the higher states of mind can be approached. You might say it is an attempt to allow the dust to settle or the clutter to get out of the way in order for clarity of vision, thought, and the organization of the contemplative mind to manifest. Meditation produces therapeutic effects in the body, such as normalizing the metabolism and lowering blood pressure (or raising it, if necessary), restoring the physical body and bringing peace into every cell. During meditation, you can monitor the body and go through it, system by system, organ by organ, part by part, to bring about a curative, healing force within it.

Meditation is the entering into the greater aspects of mind, where you come in contact with your greater self. It allows you to become one with your higher self and to overcome feelings of loneliness, grief or despair. As a vehicle for spiritual enlightenment, meditation allows you to advance by giving you some understanding of the aspects in life that are occuring, so that you may overcome your temptations and weaknesses. Meditation, therefore, can be considered a collection of yourself. Focusing your mind's eye on a singular problem or concern allows for the contemplative mind to open and allow a degree of strength, a bolt of inspiration or a revelation to occur in answer to some question or problem in life. It allows you to listen to your high self or contemplative mind and all the other dimensions that are beyond the physical world. In short, it allows you to listen to God. And through the wisdom of your soul - provided there is harmony and acceptance - meditation permits you to be guided through circumstances of your present life. In essence, it is the ability to listen to a higher force that lies beyond your conscious mind.

## *Prayer and Meditation*

In essence, prayer is the act of asking God - or any other spiritual being - for something. While prayer may be considered as seeking spiritual intervention in your life, it is through meditation that prayers are acknowledged and answers are given. As the contemplative state of meditation is an accepting state, you are better able to receive the truth, guidance and direction you seek. Too many times, however, the ego gets in the way and this simple aspect tends to be forgotten. However, meditation is, indeed, an ability to bring peace into the body and the mind, to calm the flighty emotional states, and to bring all aspects of yourself into control. It is the essence of engaging in the body's terms and conditions in order to come to some peaceful resolve. This is a state of mind that can be touched upon in which there are no dollar signs or price tags attached.

## *Effective Meditation*

The most effective way to meditate is to have clarity of mind. The body should not be tired, but it should be a little relaxed or taxed. Stretching the body, so there are no tight muscles, is a good preliminary step. The body should be voided of all waste material. Most importantly meditation is best done on an empty stomach (although a little soup is acceptable). The body should not be confined in any way. It would be best that you meditate in the same place at approximately the same time. You may dress in any manner you choose, but loose, comfortable clothing would be sufficient. There should be no physical wants or needs (i.e. thirst).

The body should be in a state of equilibrium. There should be no cares in the mind. It is not easy to allow the mind to continue thinking, but without thinking about certain things. Therefore, think about something that is nondescript and without judgment or purpose (such as a blue band or circle). Allow your mind to come out of the shell in which it has resided for most of the day. It does not wander too far away, but it returns with some invigorating emotional sensations. Your low self becomes subdued and brought in control, while your high self exudes a state of well-being, love, confidence, and unselfish giving.

## *The Practice of Meditation*

Generally speaking, meditation should only be practiced when there is time to do so, when the body is relaxed, and there is some question that needs an answer. It all depends on the purpose of the meditation: is meditation sought to relax the body and the mind; or is this an introspective meditation, in which there is some attempt to determine the cause of a health problem? As you move towards answering these questions, you will find that the purpose is more important than the practice (at least in the beginning). A suggestion would be that as you awaken each day, ask, "Dear Lord, this day is yours. What would you have me do with it?" Then follow through on what you are given. In this way, great faith will be developed. But all aspects of meditation should be contemplated.

### Deep Trance Meditation

Deep Trance Meditation is not a normal state of mind, and therefore what is occurring in this state is abnormal. The body is in a sleep-like state of relaxation or trance while another person, acting as conductor, guides the practitioner in and out of the state of meditation, directing the mind to specific things that are of concern. To some degree, the practitioner's body is asleep and the mind is very active. The heart rate is suppressed, the blood circulation is slowed, and blood pressure is lowered. The body's metabolism is under great duress or willful suppression. Blood circulates in the body but it is not cleansing itself as it should. Respiration is rather low, but all aspects of the body indeed function.

Deep Trance Meditation is simply an extension of the conscious states of meditation, during which the conscious mind is directed towards something, or is focused on something, while the deeper levels or states of mind become active. The body is put on hold and the mind is free to roam wherever it is sent. But it has conditions. The mind of the practitioner is in contact with the mind of the conductor. The conductor directs the mind of the practitioner to other minds or other things to which he or she desires. The enquiring mind visits these places and returns with information, observations or comments concerning the present state of mind. This ability to return with information from the different aspects of the ever-present moment (or the minds to which the enquiring mind is sent) is, in essence, the strength of this style of meditation or this type of communication. The mind is being sent out to observe, to understand, to gather information, and then to bring the information back, where it can be disposed of through the consciousness and vocabulary of the mind of the practitioner.

The Deep Trance method, therefore, is simply a practical application in which the mind is able to comprehend and dig into far-off objects and things without being influenced. This allows for greater clarity within the interpretation or the observation. For lighter states of meditation allow the conscious mind to be more fully aware of what is taking place within the confines of the meditation, and there is a greater chance that information becomes tainted by the conscious mind's expectations, understanding and emotions. In this method, the mind is removed and detached from the rational mind and its many influences, perspectives and interpretations, thus affording a greater degree of objectivity.

### Summary

Meditation is a very important practice. It is a religious practice. It is a spiritual practice. It is a healing practice. It is a communion practice. It aligns all of the bodies within you to a single, balanced point. It allows you to conjoin all your physical and spiritual aspects. Meditation, therefore, is a practice that allows you to touch upon the higher states of mind, and even the contemplative mind, which in itself has great ability. The states of meditation are the holiest of holies. To touch upon this state of mind is to touch upon that spark within you that is of God and from God: the soul itself.

# Chapter Ten

# DREAMS

Dreams are experiences that occur when the body is asleep and the mind continues to communicate with other minds. They are not random. Dreams are multi-leveled. Dreams are an expression of the desire for you to look within yourself and, in an introspective way, come to understand a situation or circumstance in your life. They are both literal and symbolic. They are, in fact, the language of the soul. In this regard dreams are similar to meditation, as both use sounds and images as symbols. Learning to interpret these images can benefit you greatly. Like meditation, a dream state can be a contrived, purposeful experience, and, like meditation, dreams can be considered of the future. Everything that is done in the world has been dreamed about first. In fact, it is through the states of dream that your soul can perceive greatly into the future (as well as the past and present).

There are different types of dreams: dreams during sleep, waking dreams, visions, and prophetic or revealing dreams. Dreams may also be remembrances of physical visitations or experiences in which your soul left your body to visit the spiritual dimensions. Indeed during receptive dream states, the souls of those who have gone on before you may return for the purpose of communication. A vision is simply a mental looking forward a day, two, three or whatever, and a peering into those experiences that have yet to be. Dreams and visions, therefore, being the language of the soul, are indeed forecasters of what is yet to be.

### *Mind Projection*

As the body is put to sleep and the spirit of forgetfulness overcomes the conscious mind, the subconscious mind "becomes" the conscious mind. The super-subconscious mind (or contemplative mind) "becomes" the subconscious mind. During sleep states, the mind can leave the body behind, making possible visitation to other dimensions, or other discarnate beings. This is done in order for you to be given some direction, knowledge, or understanding that you are seeking. You are able to project your soul to some distant place and to remember in the rational mind what you have experienced. This may be likened to pushing your mind forward, a process referred to as "mind projection," or "remote viewing." It is a natural state for the soul to leave the body behind during the sleep states, for in these states the body is in equilibrium, balance or peace. With the body at ease, the soul can gently leave and travel to far-off dimensions or to those who are of similar states of mind.

### *Dream Interpretation*

Being the language of the soul, dreams attempt to communicate between the high self and low self. Dreams also mitigate communication between yourself and others who are in your physical vicinity or social / family circle. The similarity between your minds draws you close together, and this coming together is a unity of mind. The high self can be described as your parental aspect, whereas the low self is your child aspect. Regardless of what it is the child wishes to do, the parent would not wish him or her to suffer, go without, or be in need. A communication between the two states of mind is established so the parent may help the child.

To prepare those states of mind for what is given from the high self to the low self, first and foremost, be prepared to record your dreams and write them down. This allows the aspects of the higher mind to begin to cooperate with your conscious mind and to communicate by answering the concerns you have or by offering hope by giving you a picture of some event that is yet to be. Once there has been some significant attempt to record - even recording that no dream took place - then you can look to your dreams in the following respects. Symbols tend to repeat. Those images in a dream which specifically capture your attention are the most important and noteworthy symbols. For instance, if you look at a clock two or three times in a row in the dream, noticing that the time is 11:45, this is of some significance. Record the symbols that repeat, and learn to interpret their meaning.

In a dream, different types of vehicles represent extensions of yourself. A sporty automobile only has room for one person to tag along, while a bus has room for a large group wishing to go in the same direction as you. In this manner, the vehicles represent how you see yourself going through life. Driving an automobile is being in charge. Sitting in the passenger seat while someone else is driving demonstrates both your willingness to cooperate, and that another person is making your choices. A motorcycle or bicycle shows that you are advancing through life on your own – in one case with a lot of power, while in the other needing a lot of effort.

Households, rooms in a house, and even the type of dwelling itself demonstrate your state of mind. The levels in the dwelling are representative of the levels of your self. The basement - filled with all its pumps, furnace and wiring - relate to the physical body. Maintenance in the basement, therefore, is also maintenance of your body. The first floor - the living room and kitchen - represent aspects in your real life or low self. The kettle represents your ability to be prepared. Being on the first floor reflects those aspects that can come into your real or physical life. The second floor relates to all aspects of your mind, for the bedrooms, hallways and chambers represent different states of mind or different consciousnesses or values within your mind. Being on the second floor demonstrates a temporal state of mind, which you would leave after giving some condolences or meeting. Rooms on the third floor represent your spiritual aspects. Typically they are demonstrative of your spiritual state of mind. If the third floor is dusty, cluttered, or not visited for long periods of time, what does this say about your spiritual self?

### *Self-Knowledge*

If you wish to gain knowledge from the dimensions beyond the physical, your dreams are the first aspect that you should approach. Dream states are controlled and natural states which you have been entering into all of your life. As there can be a gentle letting go and moving into the sleep states, and calling this up short, or going halfway, then you can enter into a deep state of knowledge and experience many things. The ability to experience such things is due to the body being at ease or asleep. Your soul naturally wants to get out of its confined space, and the soul-mind, being free to leave the body, does so. As it leaves the body, it travels, making its way through the various dimensions, depending on your will. But leaving the body is a natural occurrence. It allows you to go to the higher levels or dimensions beyond the physical to communicate with spiritual beings and to attempt to arrange events or experiences yet to be placed in your path. It also allows you to visit other individuals - or groups of individuals - who may help you in this regard. Pay attention to your dreams. Learn to interpret their messages, and you will discover that you are already receiving much guidance in your life.

# Chapter Eleven

# PRAYER

Prayer is little more than the process of repeating some thought that is held in your mind. Usually a prayer voices a desire to acquire something that you believe you need or want, but simply put, prayer is what you think about. Many people associate prayer with calling out to the spiritual beings or unseen forces that exist in the dimensions beyond the physical world. The hope is that such beings might hear your prayer, grant some relief, give some benefit, or bring some aid. In this conception, prayer is speaking to God. And it is not wrong. But prayer and meditation go hand in hand. When you pray, you are speaking to God. When you meditate, you are listening to God.

Prayer is greatly misunderstood. Often people will make conditional prayers. For example, "Dear Lord, please do something for me, and if you do, then I will do something for you." God does not bargain in this way. The prayer, "Dear Lord, if you do this one thing for me, I will be good for the rest of my life," is also a false prayer, since you can neither know, nor promise what you will be for the rest of your life. And no one would confine him or herself to such a restriction of *always* being good. Such schemes do not provoke God into doing something for you in exchange for some promise you cannot keep. In fact, they do nothing.

### How Prayer Works

To comprehend prayer is first to understand what to ask for, and then to accept it. There are many people who pray for money, asking, "Dear Lord, I need a million dollars." The trouble is, *they don't do anything to earn it.* They somewhat vaguely think that a million dollars will simply arrive on the front porch, but they do not really believe it in their minds. Prayer is a cooperative thing. You must first pray for something, and *then do everything in your power to acquire it.* Sitting at home, waiting for something to happen does nothing. You have to put yourself in a position that is conducive to the prayer being answered. If you wish to meet a mate, you might say, "Dear Lord, I wish to meet a husband (or wife). Please send that person to me as soon as possible." Now, while it is possible that someone who may become your future mate will knock on your door, it is more likely that you need to leave your house and go where other people gather. There you are more apt to meet someone with shared interests who might become your mate.

Prayer plus action equals results. Prayer is both the vocalization of something you want or need, and the action of accepting or attempting to acquire it. The great wisdom of "knock and the door shall be opened; seek and ye shall find" is indeed direction on how to use prayer. To knock on the door is to commit the prayer. To seek it out is, in essence, allowing God to provide it for you. Therefore, pray for opportunities, and for people who will bring opportunities to you. Then be willing to do anything and everything to make your prayer come about. For this, in essence, is the functionality of prayer.

There is also another old adage: "Be careful what you pray for, as you may just get it." Prayers for wisdom, patience, tolerance, or strength all bring conditions into your life that may be adverse. For in order for you to become strong, God would send adversity. This is because as you learn to solve problems, you become stronger. Exercise caution, therefore, and be specific when you commit a prayer.

### Prayer and Faith

A demonstration of good faith is the total expectation that your prayers will be answered. Faith is built upon belief and belief is built upon evidence. If you commit a prayer, and there is any doubt in your mind about your prayer coming true, then you have not committed the proper prayer, for you do not believe that it will be answered. It is human nature that when one asks for something, there is some part of him or her that does not truly believe he or she is worthy to receive it. Understand that all prayers that are committed, spoken, remembered, and said often - without any form of doubt – are answered or fulfilled in their own time. When there is doubt in your mind, it can, indeed, negate your prayer. If you pray for something and have no expectation or belief that it will be answered, then certainly it would be a waste of words and the prayer would be immediately negated. Say your prayer, believe in all your heart that it will be answered, and then do everything you can to make it happen.

### How to Pray

In making prayers for intervention, or for some result in life, it would be best to pray to yourself (or more exactly, your high self or contemplative mind). Your contemplative mind knows all that is going on in your life. It knows, before you ask a prayer, what you need, want, and will settle for. Therefore, pray to yourself not out of vanity, arrogance or conceit, but for assistance from your high self to your low self in finding your way or getting what you need. God is not your personal servant or errand-boy. God is like electricity: everywhere, ready to be utilized and ready to participate in some action. Electricity comes in many forms, from harsh lightning to harmless static electricity, but they are of the same essence. Likewise is true about prayer and to whom you should pray. Pray to your high self. Pray to the saints. Pray to the avatars and icons of your faith or religion, for these beings do exist in the world and they will assist their brothers and sisters in any way they can to relieve them of pain and want. But by praying to yourself, you involve yourself. You give your high self permission to intercede in the needs of your low self. Some people feel they are not deserving of things they want or need in life. Therefore, pray to your high self to become deserving.

Ask your high self to provide you what you need. When you look back on your life, you will always find that *what you needed* was always provided - either seemingly by chance, coincidence, circumstance or effort. Your wants sometimes were not. The difference is desperation. When you need something, you get it. You do all you can to acquire it. Your prayer constantly is for what you need, for you think about it every moment of every day. Wants are fanciful. They may come into existence, or they may not.

Therefore, pray to your high self in earnest prayer, for the high self is the part of your mind that can communicate with God (and all the other aspects of the spiritual world) to see to it that your prayer is fulfilled. Also understand that in answering prayer, God – the giver of all things – is like the ocean. You may go to the ocean to get a cup of water, or a truck-full. The choice is yours. It makes no difference to the ocean, or to God. Take as much water as you like. Pray for as much as you like. It is up to you whether you go to the ocean with a teacup or a tanker truck.

### Remember Your Prayer

When a prayer is made aloud, it is given sound, which does give it an added vibration. However, prayer is a mental process or thought process. As such, a prayer need not be uttered out loud for it to be effective. It may be simply a thought that is held in your mind. But make some symbol, or have something that reminds you that the prayer is still being made: a note on a piece of paper, a rock, a group of beads in a certain shape, a line drawn on a wall. The purpose is to remind you that you have uttered the prayer in the first place. For prayer is the process of repeating some thought that is held in your mind. A prayer forgotten is a prayer unfulfilled.

# Chapter Twelve

# EMOTIONS

Emotions are both the constructive and destructive forces within a physical body. Emotions also determine personal values of good and bad, right and wrong. They allow you to be put into various aspects of a single situation - from child to parent, from victim to victor, from abundance to nothing, and all states in between. Emotions, therefore, impact you to such a degree that they cause events and experiences in your life to be given some value, to be perceived as some sort of truth, and to give you some perspective. For memory and emotion are intricately connected. Not very often do you have one without the other. Emotion motivates or causes you to do (or not do) something. As such, the purpose of emotion is quite complex. Emotions separate humans from animals. In the animal world, emotions are raw, immediate and reactionary. Those who react emotionally are at the same low level as animals. Those who refine and define their reactions ascend to a higher level.

Emotions are part of your inner self, your being. Your soul mind or high self uses emotions to guarantee certain personality traits, responses and reactions to things that occur in your life. For it is the emotions which must be curbed, controlled, or brought into a state of peace. This is the riddle of the Sphinx. Only when all the physical (or beastly) aspects, emotional (or winged) aspects and mental (or human) aspects are brought together in a state of peace, can the fourth aspect, the spiritual (or serpentine) emanate from the pineal and pituitary glands (or the "third eye"). The emotions must be brought in line, and you must be in a state of peace or equilibrium for this to occur.

## *Motivation*

Emotions not only allow you to contemplate your past experiences and past actions, they also allow you to anticipate towards some present (or future) end, desire, or accomplishment. Emotions provide the reason, energy or fuel for you to do something: introspection, self-examination, reaction, self-control; or to move towards experiencing well-being, unity or peace in the present moment. Emotions can also motivate you to anticipate the future and overcome life's challenges, or to acquire those things of great value and pleasure. Positive stress motivates and creates. Fear causes fight or flight. Enthusiasm motivates you to great ends. Lust and greed also motivate you to accomplish great things. The emotions, therefore, can be of great benefit to you in motivating you and providing some reason for you to do something. If they are taken to extremes, however, then, indeed, emotions can work against your welfare or advancement. For extremes are difficult, and one extreme in life must be met by another.

That having been said, emotions are one of the cornerstones of yourself. They make life worth living. Emotions supply you with a greatness which allows you to overcome all the inadequacies, weaknesses, and temptations of yourself, so that you might ultimately overcome and shed all the emotions which are destructive and which retard your advancement. For the only emotion which exists beyond the physical world is love. It is the only creative emotion. When the soul progresses from the physical, material world into the higher realms, love transcends along with it. All other emotions remain behind.

### Emotions and Physical Health

Emotions can affect health in a positive way, or a negative way. Regardless of the emotion, the constant experience of it causes the body to progress, be better and healthy, or to regress, become ill and sickly. Emotions wear on your mind and attitude, thereby causing a certain expectation to exist in your mind. This expectation, reinforced or united with a certain emotion, brings about a foreseeable result or conclusion. Resentments create headaches, bowel difficulty, and constipation. Constant states of fear affect the thyroid, pancreas and the stomach. Related to fear, the continual state of worry causes stomach difficulties, such as upset stomach, or stomach ulcers. Grief and depression cause cancer. However, it is not the emotion alone that is the culprit, but when the emotion is *continuously experienced in the mind of an individual.* This causes the body to become ill or diseased. With continued experience of the emotion, it will ultimately arrive at its certain death.

Conversely, the emotions of pleasure, fulfillment and satisfaction all bring the body to a more youthful state or state of equilibrium. This keeps a body youthful, keeps a body moving and makes life enjoyable. Physical beauty, and a lack of wrinkles in the face are demonstrations of someone who does not worry, or someone who is satisfied with his or her life. A feeling of confidence and of being loved tends to keep the body strong, the back straight, and the cells in the body in good reproduction. When you have courage, you sleep better. When you have great confidence, you sleep better. But when you have peace in all things, not only do you sleep better, you live your life more fully. Bodily strength comes from self-confidence and discipline. The willingness to make yourself attractive, strong, supple or flexible requires dedication in the emotional aspects as well as the physical aspects, for the two are conjoined.

### Well-being

Throughout your life, you may work on keeping your body in good physical health, but what is most important is your state of mind. Voiding your mind of critical, harsh, or hurtful thoughts keeps your body strong, flexible and enduring. Longevity is, in effect, a state of mind sustained over the course of your life. Feelings of love, pleasure, enthusiasm, and expectation keep a body young. Remember how you felt when you caught your first fish, drove a car for the first time, or had your first kiss? How did you feel when you received your first award, won something, or achieved some personal recognition or accomplishment? For those moments in life – although fleeting - are times in which the body is lifted up to a great state of well-being, with the feeling of great joy resonating in every cell of your body. This sense of joy actually makes the cells in your body younger.

### Fear

Since negative emotions such as fear, anger and worry are potentially so harmful and destructive, why do we experience them at all? Until such time as humans can come to an understanding of the truth and learn to transcend the carnal and the temporal, we will continue to experience these emotions, for it is human nature. Each of these stem from the worst of all fears: the fear of death. This type of emotion causes two extremes in thought: flight or fight. Humans get caught up in the middle. They do not know whether to run or to stay. They attempt to do what is right and not do what is wrong, but usually they do not fully know the end result (nor do they accept the end result) of a situation or experience. This time in the middle is a period of uncertainty, of being unsure. It allows the emotion of anxiety to manifest and be experienced. Between the commencement of any event and its finality or completion, the human mind is unsure. As you aspire to the greater levels of mind, however, you begin to see the end result. All those who are prophetic, or who can see the future, or who understand expectation in the future, live a more content life. This is due to the fact that they can see the end result (or what is most likely to be). Knowing this allows you to smile and have an upbeat personality and rosy outlook, which, in turn, causes the body to be free of pain, the metabolism more perfect, and the experience of life to be much better.

As you understand how emotions can affect physical health, realize that the emotions themselves are chosen by you. It is one of the first steps that you must take: understanding and choosing not to react like an animal, but to consider what is taking place before any willful action is taken. When one animal is bitten by another, it reacts by biting back immediately, and without hesitation. Humans have the ability to be understanding: to not react in such a similar fashion, but to transcend the moment and the pain, and to be rational in what is taking place. This single ability separates humans from animals: not to react in like kind, but to be considerate and deliberate in your reactions, knowing full well that your reactions may not be proper or correct in the long run, but that they are the thing to do at that time.

You can control your emotions or how you are tricked into experiencing these emotions. And if it is such that your mind can raise up your will-power to a level at which there is a deliberate calmness about you and you are not triggered into response to any emotional state, then you have conquered or mastered the weaknesses within that would otherwise doom you to, yet again, more experiences on the wheel of life - aimlessly going again and again until you get it right.

Emotions should not be avoided. They should be looked upon as something good and welcomed, as emotions that are bottled up within may cause you great difficulty. Allow your emotions to be expelled, freely exhibited and freely utilized, as this causes you to grow and expand. As you become better able to allow emotions to be exhibited or demonstrated with tact, prudence, and agility, you will be advancing greatly. The expressed emotions free you to do other things, and to experience life to its fullest. For in a way, this is a certain kind of honesty with yourself, and this type of honesty allows you to seek only those events - or emotions - that build your character to a high degree. All others tend to hold you back.

# Chapter Thirteen

# THE PURPOSE OF LIFE

Everyone who contemplates their own existence comes to the conclusion that there must be some ultimate purpose for the various struggles of life. Why else are we made to endure them? In essence, the purpose of life is no more, no less than simply for your soul to take on a physical form and to live life in a physical world. The purpose of life, therefore, is simply to experience physical life.

Whether or not it is understood or known, each of us enters into the world to meet specific conditions and circumstances which will challenge us and help us learn the differences between construction and destruction; good and bad; advancement and retreat; and enlightenment and darkness. Physical birth is not the birth of your soul, for your soul has been in existence since the beginning. It is of God and from God. While it temporarily inhabits a physical body, it is, at all times, a soul. Between physical birth and physical death, your physical body goes through many changes. During such time, your soul has certain urgings, tendencies and conditions which it attempts to meet in order to experience all aspects of life from all different perspectives. In the end, when there have been enough life-times and your soul has experienced all the possible experiences in the physical world, then it moves on to the next level of its evolution, or to the higher realms. In the physical world, however, the purpose of engaging in physical life is to experience what it is like to live in the world.

## *Defining Your Purpose*

Each soul has a unique purpose for being here. Whether you remember it or not, while in the pre-existence your soul chose the circumstances of your present life. All souls enter into the physical world with a unique agenda and they choose a physical body which best suits this agenda. This includes physical attributes such as the size, gender, race, temperament and attitude that the body will ultimately express. In addition, the soul also makes a choice regarding the parents to which it would be born, the family and birth order within the family, as well as the physical location of the family (i.e. neighborhood, city, territory, and country). All circumstances are chosen by your soul so that you may have the best opportunity to meet the things in life you have chosen to meet.

In the pre-existence, your soul meticulously touches upon all aspects in life and "lines up" all the circumstances that will ensure a certain lifestyle. This includes consideration and choice of astrological, numerological and vibrational influences. It allows for almost a guarantee that your life will contain certain conditions, challenges, events and experiences which your soul has chosen to be meaningful or which should be encountered in your life. Your high self may choose a life of challenges, difficulties, or servitude; or it may choose one of luxury and privilege. But remember: you may be a prince in one lifetime and a pauper in the next. Your knowledge, temperament, and attitude determine the aspects, environment and specific requirements your soul desires. Those who harm in one life will be harmed in another; whereas those who help in one life will be helped in another. For by the law of karma, what is done in one experience may be undone and done to you in the next.

## *Learning to Love*

As you advance toward the greater understanding, knowledge and wisdom, you become better able to avoid temptation and destruction, and to overcome the inadequacies that are inherent within you. The ultimate purpose of the soul is to purge all extremes and the destructive and selfish tendencies so that only one tendency remains: love. Learning to love does not mean learning how to love those who are *easy to love*, but rather those who commit the most heinous crimes or bring about the most difficult circumstances to you. Learning to love these people, in spite of their transgressions, is indeed learning how to love.

Therefore, learn how to overcome all the inadequacies - both in yourself and in the world - so that there can be a love of all things in the world. Only then can you move on without regret, hatred, or any other emotion (save for love). This earthly world is a world of duality, opposites and extremes. In the dimensions beyond the physical, there is a singleness of purpose for the soul. It is to pursue the only emotion that is carried forth: unconditional love, and to be in that moment forever with unconditional love at your side.

## *The Role of Karma*

There are very unique and individual circumstances that each of us takes on to experience what our souls have freely chosen to experience. This includes the duration of physical life and how we wish to leave at the end of it. A soul may perceive all of this before it ever takes its first breath in the body it has chosen, for it knows what is best for its own progression. In the beginning, your soul chose to leave the sanctuary of the God-head to inhabit all material things and experience some physical sensation and gratification. To enter the physical world and the denseness of physical matter, it took on the density of material objects, losing the finery of its vibration and becoming a coarse and dark entity (or a fallen angel). However, there came a point of despair, and your soul recognized that there is a different way that it should go. The spirit within you allowed such introspection, followed by the motivation for your soul to move away from despair and towards love, light and life. Karma is the mechanism to accomplish this.

Many people believe that karma is some spiritual debt that is owed to another. It is better explained that karma is a debt that is owed to yourself. Debts, obligations and regrets are experienced by you, for yourself. It is through these that your soul advances or retards in its spiritual growth. For example, in one life you might be a bully, enjoying dominance and control over others to such a degree that your emotional aspects accumulate karma. This must be countered in another existence in which you are a victim: bullied and abused by another who enjoys dominance over you. In one experience, your soul witnesses the aspects of being a bully or tyrant, enjoying the position over lesser individuals. In another experience, your soul receives the bullying, living a life of fear, depression, and duress. In a third lifetime, you may find that your soul no longer wishes to be a bully or a victim. Instead, you may take on a role of authority, such as a police officer, or someone who is able to stop the bullying, punish the bully, save the bullied victim, or protect the victim from further harm. This scenario represents three aspects of the same circumstance. There are other points of view as well: the parents of both the bully and the victim, those in the judicial system, educators, friends of both the bully and the victim, and other casual observers who witness the bullying (and who either chose to react or not). The soul attempts to understand all these different perspectives. It may choose to enter each of these roles individually and record the experience in its own mind, or it may be wise enough to observe only two or three perspectives. The more that your soul understands, and the less willing it is to enjoy causing pain or suffering, the less it needs to spend time in these different perspectives, going over the lessons from all these different points of view. As such, you can move on to the next level of observation and education, adding to the record of your soul what is preferred and correct and what is not preferred and not correct.

The current understanding of karma is that if you hit another at one time, you will be hit back at another. This indeed may be true. But if you hit someone while defending yourself or your family, then it is correct that you cause harm to another. After all, the intruding person seeks to inflict suffering and to destroy. As a member of your family willing to do so, it is your duty to prevent this from happening. However, if you *enjoy* causing great pain to the perpetrator, then you will pick up some of this karma and it will become owed to you. But if you treat it as simply matter-of-fact, then there is no karma (nor a need to continue). It is simply a duty that must be carried out. This is likewise true in the other extreme. If you take action with guilt or regret, then this, too, builds a certain karma, causing the need for you to engage in this experience again, in order to understand the truth and not feel guilty, regretful or remorseful. If you can act with as much compassion and understanding as you can, without being impassioned or feeling any desire or enjoyment, but simply carrying out your duty, then you will be in a situation of equilibrium and neutrality of emotion. This allows you to move on without fear of retribution or "bad karma." In doing this, therefore, your soul meets the conditions that it has chosen to meet. As the soul gains an understanding, it is able to move on.

### Other Forms of Karma

Should you procrastinate and avoid some circumstance, or make a mistake, then you become doomed to repeat the same experience over and over again until you get it right. If you notice that the same circumstance presents itself again and again in life, then usually the correct way is to do what you are afraid to do (or do not wish to do). Indeed, learning can be a challenging and difficult experience, but taking the easy way out lessens the importance of the lesson in the first place. Therefore, when difficulty comes your way, embrace it fully. Look deep within yourself to see what is going on. What are the lessons here? What is the challenge? Where do you feel threatened? Face these phantoms – and the sooner, the better - so that you might learn your lesson.

### Mistake and Willful Commitment

If you cause harm or damage unwittingly or by mistake, and you never repeat it again, then this can be considered a learning step. For to make an error or a mistake demonstrates your willingness to learn. It may also be seen as a stepping-stone to your success, for stalling, retreating or turning away at the threshold of success usually dooms you to repeat the circumstance again. Therefore, do not be afraid of making mistakes, *but do learn from them*, as this will accelerate you to the greatest degree of success. Being aware of this, however, puts you into a precarious situation, for if you do something that you know is willfully wrong - and then willfully do it again - the penalty you pay will be even greater. If what you do is an error or mistake, you may feel embarrassed, and you may need to apologize or make restitution monetarily, but the karma ends there and you can move on. On the other hand, if what you do is knowingly or wantonly known to be incorrect or wrong, then you may face graver issues than apology or embarrassment. Your very wealth, health and life may be held in jeopardy.

Understand that the subconscious knows no value, and as such, harm given to yourself is done without emotion. If it is a matter that you should have learned something or overcome something in a different way, and it is necessary for you to be given out some punishment or retribution, your subconscious can easily put yourself in harm's way. This is the rule that karma plays. It is like having an umpire or referee inside your mind. It plays the game fairly, knows the rules of intervention and intrusion, and puts you in positions where retribution or revenge would be carried out at your own hand. When you wantonly and knowingly go against what you know is correct, or when a little correction is necessary, some hardship, difficulty, and disappointment may be set up in your life. This is done from within, fairly and in an impartial manner, without exaggeration.

# CHAPTER THIRTEEN

This is the role the karmic influences play: setting up circumstances in your life that are pertinent to the lesson you are attempting to learn. When you witness the same problem coming up again and again in your life, do something totally different (which is usually the most difficult thing to do) and you will meet your karma and learn your lesson, negating the necessity to engage in these circumstances again. When you understand this, then you become more willing to meet the challenges and the most difficult circumstances in life, knowing that, by meeting these conditions, your soul advances greatly.

The same holds true for pleasurable and abundant things in life. Learning how to handle great material wealth is, indeed, a challenge and can cause as much duress as having no money. Karma is a great, balancing, universal law that none can escape, for it is the responsibility of every person to move forward on his or her own accord. No one can do it for you. When you understand this, your sense of duty and purpose allows you to willingly meet those things that you must meet, regardless of how pleasurable or how distressing. Have faith that you will never be given more than you can handle, for God is a loving and just God. If you genuinely repent or regret, any karmic debt that is owed would be instantly removed. Through the Law of Grace, you need not experience those conditions of grief or difficulty, for you will have already learned your lesson. This is the purpose of life, for knowledge plus experience equals wisdom. To be within your life's purpose is to demonstrate your willingness to be (or get) back on track, and to overcome life's distractions and temptations, headed towards the great enlightenment or self-recognition and realization.

## Destiny and Free Will

Each of us possesses free will and free choice. In the beginning, souls were together in the God-head. When they became aware that they possessed free will and free choice, those who chose to do so left this sanctuary and went out into the universes to explore and examine the material aspects. They did this of their own free will and accord. At some time, they decided to return to the sanctuary, although they did not know how to return. For through their physical gratification, their vibration from purity was lessened, tainted or stained. To return to the God-head, your soul must experience certain things. In order for you to engage in a certain "plan," or set of circumstances which will allow you to experience what your soul needs to experience, you engage in certain actions in life. This may be considered as your destiny. These circumstances, trials or challenges must be met in your life. There is no getting around, belittling or reducing them. Therefore these are part of your destiny. It is your duty to meet these challenges or these things, and indeed the sooner, the better. No one else but you is able to carry out this activity.

Briefly put, your destiny is made up of the things that are going to happen to you, regardless of what you do. You may not escape the circumstances, trials or challenges in life. Free will is the willingness to do those things that you choose to do. Using free will, however, you cannot escape your destiny. For free will or free choice is such that you may rush into a particular circumstance and meet it head-on, rather than procrastinate, whine and cry, or substitute someone else to do your bidding. For in essence, being an individual, you must engage in certain practices and activities that allow you to advance in your spiritual evolution.

For example, if it is your destiny to work in construction and save the life of another worker, then your destiny would be given out in the construction world. In going to a construction site, you can freely choose to be an electrician, truck driver, carpenter, laborer, or some other tradesperson. But on that particular day, at that particular time, in meeting your destiny, you will be working as some form of construction worker in a construction setting. Then you will meet the circumstance: whether or not to save the life of another. It does not really matter if you are a plumber, electrician or carpenter. What does matter is that you help another and you are in the circumstance you have chosen, which was to be a construction worker.

Another way of looking at the interplay between destiny and free will is to consider what happens when you compose a letter. The certain points that you wish to be made in the letter represent your destiny. After all, the purpose of writing the letter is for these points to be made. Free will and free choice may be looked upon as how the letter is laid out: the forming of sentences, the grammar, and the punctuation. Whether the three or four points would be made chronologically, mixed up, all at the beginning, or all at the end of the letter is your choice. But regardless of how they are made, you will make those points in the letter.

To some degree, this is a simplified explanation of the difference between free will, free choice and destiny. But try as you might, destiny must always be met. The willingness to meet your destiny is a demonstration of your faith, for you will never be given anything more than what you can bear. Have faith in this, and be prepared to meet your destiny head-on. The willingness to meet those difficulties usually allows you a greater advantage: to seek the ways and means to avoid difficulty or find solutions to problems in life you are attempting to solve.

### *Discover Your Destiny*

In order to discover your own destiny, first be patient. Remember that your primary destiny is to live life in a physical world, not to be concerned with what might be, nor with far-off confrontations or circumstances. Look around you and at what is close at hand. You may see your destiny. It may unfold day by day. Ultimately it may arrive at some far-off point in time. For some people, the purpose in life is revealed to them, and they can see the end part of their lives. As they look back, they can see the road taken and the steps or choices they made which allowed them to arrive at such a point in time. A way to discover your destiny is to imagine yourself in a different time, far ahead. Picture an older version of yourself looking back on what was accomplished. As you do this, you may perceive circumstances or activities which give you some hint as to the ultimate conclusion in your physical life - or perhaps a possibility of what is taking place in your physical body and this worldly experience.

Choosing to meet your destiny is choosing to be productive and to work as if your life depended upon it, as if God were your boss and the only one you needed to please. Work towards a worthwhile goal. But also look at what types of mistakes you are making over and over again. Attempt to correct these mistakes so that you come to your ultimate conclusion. If you can't balance your check-book, for example, and you have great difficulty handling money, then learn how to handle money, how to balance your check-book, and how to put yourself on a budget. If you are having difficulty with authority, then learn how to become an authority and how to relate to someone who is under authority. In other words, move towards things that are difficult, for they tend to draw you out to become greater than you are.

Through states of meditation or dream, your future will be revealed to you: what you would be or could be. After all, it is already within your mind. The difficulty is in attempting to remember this. In states of contemplation or meditation, or though the asking of prayer, there can be a revelation to you of what you will become. But remember that you may be a welder, truck driver, carpenter or electrician. Regardless of what you choose, if your ultimate vocation is to work in construction, it makes little difference what you choose. But choose to be content or happy at your vocation. Find ways and means to do work that is enjoyable or playful. In so doing, you will meet your destiny in such a way that there would be great joy in your life.

Everyone's destiny is simply to experience physical life. Start with this in mind. Secondly, contribute to the world. Stand up to the strong when they are in the wrong. Always do right, and obey your conscience. These are stepping-stones leading to the ultimate revelation of what you will become, without guilt and with satisfaction or purpose in your conscious mind. If you can choose a single pathway (and it is your destiny to be what you have chosen), then get on it right away. Experience it to the fullest degree and you will meet your destiny. Do not be afraid to make mistakes, for as you go through the experiences of your life, you may change the approach to your destiny. It makes little difference in the end.

## Look For Clues

Consult all the information, holy men, influences, numbers and stars, and draw from this a great picture of your tendencies, understandings, strengths and weaknesses. This will help you see your future, and to see what you are geared for, destined for, or best equipped to become. Seek and you will find your destiny. There are many clues as to what you will become. But draw on your feelings to aim at something that is enjoyable and will make you feel proud. Go after this with all your heart, mind and energy, and realize that you will get there somehow. Perhaps you will not be the pilot of an aircraft. Perhaps you will be the co-pilot, navigator, flight attendant or maintenance worker. But there you will be, meeting your destiny to work on an airplane. In time, you will define what level or what position you are best suited for. But let enthusiasm guide you into a field of endeavor or vocation. As you seek within, and you ask for guidance, you will be given information so that you may ultimately fulfill your destiny. Look to the clues that are around you, from all the input or information there is, bearing in mind that you should always be prudent and patient. Then your destiny will shine through. Keep in mind that your unique destiny may be simply to be present at a certain place, and at a certain time to accomplish a certain thing. Don't try too hard to find your destiny. It will eventually find you.

### *Attitude*

The purpose of life is to experience physical life and enjoy it to the greatest degree, while meeting all the challenges that come towards you, with the faith and knowledge that God would not send anything greater than what you can bear. When a challenge - or a blessing - comes to you, know that it is always temporal, for in physical life everything comes to pass. While difficulties may live in your mind for the rest of your life, they last only a moment. Purge your mind. Overcome difficulties as quickly and as easily as you overcome the joyfulness of an exciting carnival ride: scary as you go through it, exhilarating as you overcome it, and once it is over, you can leave it in the past with a memory of accomplishment. Humans tend to hang on to those things that are destructive. They go over and over them in their minds. This, in all essence, stops the mind and imprisons it in time. The purpose of physical life is to experience things sweet and sour, good and bad, exciting and dull, *and then to move on*. Picture a bird nesting in a tree. When the temperature drops below freezing, it may freeze to death. In a moment, it is rejuvenated and does not freeze, or in a moment it falls prey to the bitter cold and dies. Whatever the outcome, it doesn't complain much for the rest of the day. It accepts what has come upon it, and it moves on to its next experience, whether bitter or pleasurable, exhilarating or dull. It chooses to live for the moment and to anticipate the next moment without leaving its mind several moments behind.

Let this become part of your understanding of how to meet physical life and to experience it. Dwell more on the good times and the good people in your life than those times that were filled with despair or difficulty. Everyone meets the challenge of physical life every morning. They must rise up and struggle with the day. Their attitude determines how the day turns out. When it rains, a wise person says, "My, today I get to experience working in a rainstorm." One who is unwise might say, "The day is ruined because of that damned rain!" Which one is embracing life and moving forward? Obviously the second.

Therefore, let your attitude always be "My, I *get* to experience something," and your entire attitude, state of being, and state of peace will change. "My, I get to experience what it is like to mend a broken arm. If God has chosen this for me, then I will experience what it is like to have a broken arm and what it is like to mend it. And I will experience it greatly." This attitude changes you and allows you to meet those conditions in life that may be difficult, and greatly challenging to you. But by meeting the challenge, you will have experienced life to its fullest and you will have experienced life from many perspectives. Then not only will you be able to move on to a more joyous experience in physical life, but your soul will be able to move to a more enlightened state. For your soul has chosen to enter the world at this point in time. How are you going to live your life to make the world a better place? Make your life a better life and make the things in your life more joyous. By doing so, you will change the entire outlook of the world and, therefore, the destinies of all. For if one changes his or her mind, then all are changed. As you come to understand this, you will understand the power of physical life and the power of choosing a mind that seeks to meet those things that the soul has chosen for it to meet. For this life is but one breath in the life of the soul. And if the soul lives forever, there really is no hurry.

# Chapter Fourteen

# LIVING A LONG LIFE

### *The Immortal Human Soul*

As discussed previously, emotional states are both the constructive and destructive forces of the body, and things that are held in the mind are manifested in the body. The mind, therefore, is both the builder and the way. Humans struggle for most of their existence to come to some resolve at controlling themselves emotionally and mentally. The spirit within is the force or ability that attempts to do this. The spirit is the force that causes you to examine yourself, both in the present moment and in reflection of those moments past. It is a demonstration of your spirituality. Humans are the only animals capable of reflection and introspection. We contemplate what has happened and what will happen. We look back from the present moment to the past – even to the distant past, beyond our own life-times, or those of our ancestors. We also look forward from the present moment to our immediate future, ultimate future, and to the future or legacy that lies beyond the present life-time. This, again, is a demonstration of that force that is within - your spirit - reflecting upon the causes and purposes of the soul.

The key to physical longevity is to understand the immortality of the human soul; the consequence of this immortality being the value of physical life. From the perspective of your conscious mind, this life is all that exists. But from your soul's perspective, your present life is but one breath in the life of the soul. It is but one, brief experience in order to express those things that you are attempting to learn, understand, or add to yourself for the advancement of your soul to its greatest and ultimate realization. This is the Christ consciousness, or to touch upon the God-head while in the physical and spiritual states.

To achieve physical longevity, you must understand that your conscious mind needs to adhere to positive, constructive emotions and peace of mind. For following the dictates of the constructive emotions and constructive states of mind will allow you to accomplish longevity of the body by maintaining its optimum health. What is held in the mind is always brought about in the physical body. It is not the other way around. Therefore your attitude, thinking, contemplation or mental aspects are, indeed, the light that shines into the darkness of an uncertain future. This light illuminates the way to longevity and to all aspects of God: health, wealth and peace of mind.

### Balance is the Key

The key to longevity is to attempt to keep yourself in a state of balance, peace and pleasurable (but non-carnal) expectation. You must learn to discipline yourself by putting limits on all desires, seeking reward rather than failure, and by learning that fear is crippling (as it robs you of your peace). If you can come to a state of mind in which you are willing and accepting, then you will have great faith. Realize that faith is built upon belief, and belief is built upon evidence, one step at a time. Your faith would be held strongly in the belief that no matter what comes upon you, God would not give anything that would be too much for you to bear. There is never a problem or difficulty that will come into your life that will not have a solution. As long as you are willing to overcome adversity and the difficulties in life and seek a peaceful way (whenever possible) in all things, then you will develop a great sense of peace of mind which will carry you forward through any difficulty you encounter.

In the long view, you must meet those things – the challenges or difficulties - that are, in essence, the making of things you have done in previous experiences. Once again it is a case of "self meeting the self" in the present moment. Understanding this allows you to have a simple faith to put a limit on all your physical appetites. If, at all times, you are ready and willing to engage life for self-improvement, then when you make a mistake and correct yourself from that mistake, you progress greatly. For regret wipes out karmic debt. To sin is simply to err, or to be off the mark. In archery terms, to sin is to miss the target; whether it is slightly or greatly is of no consequence. What does matter is that you try to get back on the path, the mark, or the line that takes you directly to the target. In so doing, you will not feel guilty, nor harbor feelings of adversity or criticism towards yourself. For criticizing of oneself is criticizing that which is within: the soul itself. As the soul is of God and from God, then criticizing oneself is criticizing God. And criticizing God is sinful indeed.

### Attitude and Emotions

Be willing to make mistakes. By doing so, you are willing to learn. Once you learn what is right, then you willingly and promptly change yourself to do what is right. If this means to eat a proper diet, to exercise the body thoroughly, to wash the body externally as well as internally, and also to wash the mind of those fragments or barbs that may come into it, then you will be willing to keep your heart pure and your mind optimistic. You will experience a gladness to endure physical life for a longer period of time. For the attitude is the way. The attitude is the key. For example, you might say, "My God, it is raining hard out there today. Oh, I am going to have a miserable day because of this darned rain." For the rest of the day, you are depressed, angry, frustrated, resentful, bitter, irritable and hard to get along with. Another person might say, "My, look how hard it is raining! Today I am going to have a great day. The rain has come to wash the planet clean, and make the plants grow. Today I am going to have a great day."

When your attitude is immediately shifted from despair to optimism, the creative aspects within yourself become highly elevated. There is a sense of being in harmony with the environment. More importantly, this is a demonstration that you are not controlled from without, but from within. For does the weather really control how you should feel? No. *You* choose how to feel, for each of us possesses free will and free choice. Choosing to feel upset causes the glands in your body to react adversely. Choosing to feel optimistic, on the other hand, causes the glands to operate positively and creatively. Even at the cellular level, your body is affected by attitude. The body is not divided into several islands - each one distinct, separate, disjointed and disconnected from the next. On the contrary. Every cell of the body is conjoined. Every organ is affected by the other. When you are in a state of well-being or love, your entire body chemistry changes. To be in a state of love is to be in the highest possible state of ecstasy, creativity and longevity-producing hormones, activities, currents, or flows in the body. To be in a state of fear, self-condemnation, or worry is the opposite. The constructive emotions build the body, whereas the destructive emotions tear it down. Fear and worry are destructive; enthusiasm and peace are constructive. The most constructive emotion of all is love.

A key to comprehending the emotions and mental states is to understand that enthusiasm can guide you through all aspects of life, lighting the way through that darkened room towards positive, constructive, and peaceful activities and emotions which build the body up. Resentment, hatred, frustration and worry, likewise, tear the body down. Each body is prepared and capable of reproducing cells throughout the entire body. Once in every cycle, the entire body has been replaced from top to bottom with new cells, for cells in the body are constantly being generated and old cells are being replaced and discarded. It would make sense, therefore, that the body should perpetuate a state of health, and well-being, since all cells of the body are continually being replaced by new ones. How, then, can it be that the body ages, suffers disease and becomes decrepit? In essence, it is due to the mind, the personality and the emotions associated with life - things that are held in the mind as fears, worries, and resentments in particular. The destructive emotions affect the vibration of the cell such that old cells are replaced not with new, vibrant cells, but with cells that have been tainted by the vibration of the emotion to which the body resigns itself, accepts, or perpetuates. One who lives in a state of worry perpetuates this daily.

Understand that your mind was designed to be chaotic and random, examining many things throughout the day. It is an error to be focused on any one thing for a long period of time. Sometimes when you make a mistake, your mind freezes at that point in time. You never forget making the mistake, nor do you learn to forgive yourself. You are, in fact, stuck at a moment of time that is rapidly receding further into the past. Some would call this grief, guilt, or regret. But daily maintaining a mental focus on that same point tends to hold a body back and causes it to prematurely age. Similarly, repressed anger and resentment causes internal pressure, affecting the circulatory system. When pressures become so high, the blood vessels and heart dilate or expand to the point of bursting.

To counter this, experience a sense of enthusiasm, hope, love, and joy as often as possible. This will counteract the thoughts that cause dis-ease in the body. The other emotions are justifiable and acceptable in their own time and place, and they do need to be expressed from time to time. But tending to keep your mind towards the positive or constructive emotions is also the key to keeping the body and its healing processes functioning for longevity in the physical body.

### *Maintaining the Body through its Years*

The body needs regular maintenance, exercise, sleep, and prayer; a balance of work, rest, nourishment and spiritual sustenance. A rule of thumb for longevity is keep balance in all things. Eat a little of all types of food. Do all sorts of things that keep bringing newness into your life. Don't worry about worry. Move on from a point of difficulty or other such situation in which you find yourself. And remember that those brief moments of glory, pride, success, and public acceptance will, indeed, be brief. Enjoy them to the fullest, therefore, but realize that all things in life come to pass. By accepting that all things come to pass, you can gracefully age through the years. For in essence, life is movement. In the beginning, the cells are vibrant and movement of the body is swift. Children run for the sake of running. They enjoy movement. From the beginning of life towards the end, there is a gradual slowing down of the physical body. But again, the physical body becomes slower because the mental activities and emotions become slower (or duller). Keep yourself lively and your life full. Let there be an expectation of wonder for all the days of your life. This is the key to successful enjoyment of good health through long years of life. As your body gets older, always let your mind demonstrate a sense of wonder, youthfulness, and enthusiasm.

Then tend to the mundane or physical level. Consume plenty of water. Eat many varieties of vegetables and eat those things that are old in nature. Consume a small amount of all types of food, rather than eating a lot of similar foods. Turtle eggs have a tendency to add vitality. Water that is high in alkalinity also helps the body to age gracefully. As the body practices eliminations in all respects, then it will remove the sedentary forces or sediments, toxins and poisons that have built up within it over the years. As such, the body will better maintain physical purity and perfection. What tends to make the body sluggish in all its activities are the toxins that creep into it and become stored in the body's "nooks and crannies." Keep the body moving. Breathe deeply. Keep the blood cleansed as much as possible. Stimulate the lymphatic system through physical exercise or manual manipulation (massage) so that its movement is good. But eliminations are key.

## *Reversing the Degenerative Effects of Old Age*

Can old age be reversed? Well, it depends. If your body is decrepit and in great difficulty, it may be too late for you to attempt a complete reversal in your physical condition. But the body *always* has the ability to improve its state of health, or lessen the burden of years that have come upon it. If you have abused your body over the years, you should not expect it to respond quickly. However, with regard to the normal wear and tear on the body, if you attempt to maintain your body throughout your life, then you can age gracefully and slow down the aging process. For instance, attempting to keep the blood vessels flexible, pliable, and elastic is a key to longevity and youthfulness. But in order to do this, the body must be worked hard so that the blood pressure would fluctuate up and down. When you run around the block, for instance, your blood vessels flex as the internal pressure increases in order to pump the blood quickly throughout the body and into the skin. As the blood rushes through all parts of the body, delivering oxygen as fuel for living cells and removing by-products and waste to be disposed of in a more useful way through the blood vessels, the body becomes invigorated, refreshed, and renewed. This simple act of keeping the blood vessels flexible prevents hardening of the arteries from taking place. It also prevents plaque and other build-up on the walls of the arteries (which causes restriction of blood flow). This causes the body to deliver good, nourishing, oxygen-rich blood throughout the entire body. When there is hardening of the artery, or the building up of plaque, which causes restriction in the artery, the organs and extremities are denied of blood. Not only would disease occur, but eventually death.

This simple act - this simple practice of keeping the arteries flexible, pliable or elastic - will add years to your life and keep a high quality of physical life. It makes no difference whether you use absorbing oils to affect the arteries, or doing regular physical exercise that causes expansion and contraction on a regular basis (or some combination of the two). *But do something.* Many already know this, yet how many pay attention before it is too late? It is something that should be worked on all of your life. However, when plaque build-up and hardening of the arteries or sedentary forces begin to show themselves, then immediate action needs to be taken. To rectify the condition and remove the sedentary forces in the body, use massage, chelation therapy, and teas that would cleanse the body, or stimulate the kidney, liver, bladder and spleen. This would also remove diseases within the body that have resulted from viral, bacterial and parasitic conditions.

### *Foods for Longevity*

In essence there is really no bad food (provided that it is natural). Now, food that is manufactured or processed tends not to be good for the body. Food that is gathered from the vine, dug out of the ground, or plucked from the plant as leaves are the best. Food should be gathered from the vicinity or region in which the body resides, and it should be of the freshest variety. Vegetables should be eaten within hours of being harvested, as after about four or six hours, the vitality of the plant begins to lessen. Ultimately you are left with the bulk of the dead plant, the vitality lessened or completely lost. Foods that are processed with added sugar, salt or fat should be avoided, therefore. Eat a little of all the plants. Each day there should be one from below the ground and three from above. Of the three from above the ground, two should be of the leafy variety, the other of the bean or pod. Head lettuce should not be eaten, as it is largely useless. Vegetables should be of the freshest variety, and grown within the vicinity in which you reside. If meats are to be eaten, it would be better to consume fish, fowl and lamb - baked, boiled or broiled – than to eat pork (although a little crisp bacon from time to time would not hurt). You should also consume plenty of water - four to ten glasses each and every day. Water that is high in minerals is preferable to water that has been bleached, blanched, steamed or distilled.

As a rule of thumb, try not to eat foods singularly and repetitively. Too much of anything is not a good thing. If you eat a little of all the berries, for example, they would do you a service. But if you constantly eat only strawberries, it tends to imbalance the body and you would become ill. Therefore, the body should be encouraged to eat as many foods as it can possibly find. Try not to eat a small number of foods as your mainstay in life, for one excess in life tends to breed another.

### *"After breakfast, work a while..."*

It has been said that a good rule of thumb for living is after breakfast, work a while; after lunch, rest a while; and after supper, walk a mile. Indeed, the best time to work your body is in the morning. When is it that the birds and animals are most active? It is in the time just prior to, during, or just after the dawn. Be like the birds. Morning is a time of awakening. It is a cheery time, and a time of great enthusiasm. This is the best time to get your body moving, for during the dormant state of sleep, you have engaged in a replenishing and renewing of the physical body. In the morning, you awake, as if from a death-like state. In essence you are reviewing, renewing and invigorating yourself. It is also during this time that the body is most able and capable to work. Therefore, work hard during the morning. Let the morning meal be the greatest or largest meal of the day (or the meal with the most fat). A body can work well from the early morning through to midday.

The meal at midday replenishes what has been expelled, used up, or worked off during the physical exertion of the morning. After this, a little rest or nap at midday - which is the hottest time of the day - would also replenish what the body has used up in the morning. Then after you re-awaken from this rest and work again in the latter part of the day, the evening meal would be taken. Afterwards, the body would need some form of exercise, away from its normal work. Walking is the best form of exercise, for all systems in the body can be in harmony, and all organs can be taxed pleasurably. The rhythm causes the body's digestion and elimination to function more correctly. As such, this constitutional walk allows the organs and eliminative functions of the body to be greatly enhanced or improved. This walk also allows the body to settle down. It is a pleasurable time, a rhythmic time in which the body and the conscious mind are engaged in the act of walking and the contemplative mind (that part of the mind that transcends the physical aspects) begins to contemplate the nature around you. This enhances your breathing and it prepares the body for sleep. Then the body is ready to begin the cycle again. The body has been thoroughly worked in the morning; it has avoided the strong rays of the sun by resting and recuperating in the middle of the day; and in the evening a sense of maintenance is brought in with the walk, permitting the digestive and eliminative forces in the body to be brought to bear without the exertion of the work that has gone on in the morning. While the daily work may be repetitive and strenuous, the evening walk is therapeutic (as is the nap in the middle of the day). For some people it is better to exercise in the early morning, while others would prefer late at night. It makes little difference, but it is better to exercise *at any given time of the day* than not to exercise at all.

## Life in a World of Duality

Life can be a joy, or it can be a struggle. Certainly life is filled with great difficulty, for the physical world is a place in which duality is one of the purposes of physical life. You live in duality, between the two pillars or extremes of good and evil, ease and difficulty. Accept this and embrace this place as a place of duality. Understand that physical life is little more than experiencing what it is to be in the physical world in a physical body, experiencing all aspects of physical life. Depending on your perception, you either wish to live a longer life, or you grope for ways and means to end it. Whether or not it is understood or believed, *you alone make the choice when to leave this world* and the manner in which you do so.

Therefore, if you wish to live a long life, it would seem logical that you would have some reason for wanting to do so. In choosing to live a long life, first let the spirit within you determine the reason why you would want this to happen. Then do everything in your power to make this happen. Always move forward towards this goal: your reason for long life. Then be prepared to work at it, and put into place the things you deem necessary and prudent for long life. Allow these things you hold true to prevail over all the temptations and extremes in life, without exception. If this is done, then you may be well on your way to a long and enjoyable life.

Physical life holds a purpose for your soul. The soul advances, based on the experiences and understandings it obtains or comes to hold as true in this life. While your soul is going through these challenges, lessons, or purposes, it is permitted to enjoy the trip - as well as the arrival at the destination. Plan your life, and be prudent and practical in all aspects of it. It may seem a little boring that life needs to be planned, but if you can do this, then, indeed, life will be easier, and all aspects of longevity can manifest themselves. Have respect for your physical body. It is the temple of your soul. Reverence of the physical body is a demonstration of reverence for the immortal soul within.

The rules, therefore, are simple. Choose to live a long life. Choose to have a purpose for living this long life. Then choose all things that are beneficial in order that you may enjoy a long and healthy life. Allow your mind and attitude to always find things of enthusiasm, or things that make you feel good inside. When trouble comes your way - whether it is a challenge or a criticism - allow yourself to accept those difficulties with the same enthusiasm as you would feel with anything else. Overcoming these difficulties makes you strong and great of spirit. Do not run from life's challenges. Embrace them openly and fully. Drink deeply from the cup of despair, if it is given to you. But, likewise, drink deeply from the cup of success when it is offered, as well. Maintain balance in all things. Take responsibility for yourself. Always choose light and life. Be true to yourself and honor what you know is right. Then you will find within yourself that burning sensation to live life to its fullest.

# Chapter Fifteen

# RELATIONSHIPS AND SOUL-MATES

## *Romantic Longing*

In each of us, there is a yearning, desire, or longing to come together with someone else to form a bond of affection and love. As souls, we enter into the physical world with strengths and weaknesses. We seek to overcome the weaknesses in ourselves and our feelings of loneliness, incompleteness and imperfectness, by seeking a romantic partner. When two people come together, a blending occurs as the strengths of one partner complement the weaknesses of the other. For in the finite, physical world, it is the very nature of opposites to come together. As they do, a union takes place and the two halves become whole, or one. Also out of this pairing comes some result: it may be the creation of a new life, or it may be a modification in the lifestyles of the two partners, causing an increase in their lives. It is a function of nature that two souls, coming together for completeness, result in something larger than the two on their own.

When they are together, the two partners of a couple learn from one other and they spiritually advance. Now, it is usual that one will advance a little faster than the other. However, as he or she turns to the other partner and reaches out to pull the other up a little, then the union blossoms and the couple participates in greater spiritual and physical experiences (provided they both advance or grow together). At this level, you cannot attract anyone who is far greater or lesser than yourself, for on the mental and spiritual levels, like attracts like. Similar and linked, the two attach or come together on the physical and spiritual levels to progress to the greatest states of mind that they are capable of, for the advancement of their very souls.

## Soul-mates

What are soul-mates? Simply, these are binary souls which come together for a period of time to interact with one other in a romantic and loving way. Throughout the ages, they continue to come in contact with each other, in a regular, yet intermittent way, looking for one another as they enter into the physical world. It can be also understood that soul-mates are just souls that interact with each other. You might say they have formed an alliance together in the pre-existence, and they are concerned with one other's advancement or welfare, to some degree. As individual spiritual beings who come together from time to time, soul-mates share a certain level of comfort, knowledge and understanding with each other that is very intimate and deep, not requiring any explanation or expression. They need not come into the physical world together at the same time, in the same circumstances or in the same relationship. They can go for several millennia in different directions or to different dimensions to encounter experiences for their own enlightenment or advancement. But from time to time, for their own reasons, they do choose to enter into the physical world at the same time. As binary souls, souls that have become attached to one other and have some meaningful relationship with one other, each soul relies upon the other to advance itself through difficult life-times, difficult circumstances, or through life in general. As they advance, each relies upon the other for all of its material needs while on the earth – including the carnal aspects - and for association and support in the dimensions beyond, so there may be advancement to the higher levels of consciousness. In assisting one another in this way, each soul may progress through the higher levels of unconditional love to touch upon the source of pure love itself: the God-head.

Unlike the finite, conscious mind, the contemplative mind or soul mind has memory of all things that it has encountered. When each soul comes across the other - either by design or by chance – it remembers (without consciously remembering or acknowledging) the details of the other and their previous experiences and life-times together. It is a profound experience. There is an intimate and sudden recognition that goes beyond what usually happens at a chance meeting. You may have an instant rapport or feel as though you have known one another for years. Indeed, this is because your souls have known each other for many years.

In some life-times, soul-mates wait to find each other to carry out certain aspects of their progression. In other life-times, they simply touch upon one another for brief periods, assisting each other, if necessary, and then moving on, after accepting that the other is getting along in the circumstances it chose to take upon itself. But understand that at any time they need to contact one another, there can be mind-to-mind communication through the higher levels or states of mind. They need not always come together to touch upon one another in the physical world.

This said, however, from time to time soul-mates do touch upon one another *because they love one another.* They love one another so much that they are able to separate from one another to advance through the levels of consciousness. This can be done only on their own merit, responsibility and cognizance, as they attempt to touch upon the greater consciousness, or the God-head. They seek enlightenment to aid and help one another, but each soul realizes that the other must advance on its own accord. If one tarries or fails, the other usually does not wait, but continues on.

In the spiritual levels beyond the physical world, there is no jealousy, hatred, or possessiveness. There is simply affection, for love is the only emotion that transcends this dimension (in which all these other emotions reside). On the dimensions that await the soul, love is shared with one and with many. Soul-mates have the capability to love many with the same intensity and to the same extent that they love the one. Therefore, alliances such as this should not be seen in the singular, but in the multitude.

## *Your Soul-mate*

If you are seeking your perfect match - a mating of mind and soul - you must always aspire to be greater in your own enlightenment and in your search for God. For both you and your soul-mate not only have the fiduciary responsibility to assist one another to the higher realms or levels, but you each must take the steps to do so yourselves. Do not conceive of this as co-dependency, but rather co-operation, each soul-mate assisting the other, realizing that it must move forward on its own, above and beyond all that it has come into the world to overcome. In doing so, each can have a satisfying, deep, rich, emotional affection for the other – and one that is so much that they do not possess one other. For pure, unconditional love is not possessive.

But even on the spiritual level, there is a completeness. When the two hearts and minds and the two genders come together, there is a spiritual unity, such that they are indistinguishable from one another. Whether there is male and female gender of body, or male and female gender of soul, it makes little difference, as long as there is balance, or the accumulation of the two becoming one. For in essence, the two *must* come together to make themselves whole, for without the other, there is a sense of being incomplete. It is not necessary to advance through life as a couple, however. One can have several short-term affairs or "excursions" and still fulfill oneself by oneself.

However, there is the tendency that when the two partners come together, they provoke each other to grow more. When the situation is intimate - such as being part of a couple, union, or friendship - there can be no deception or façade. Each person begins to know the other so much that they are stripped away of all their layers of protection or armor, and they are left naked. When you are part of a couple, you cannot mask your own thoughts and feelings, and, therefore, you must communicate to your partner. Provided there is a will to be enlightened, and you both attempt to do so, you will grow faster together. If you simply come together for all the amenities of a physical relationship, existing in the world in a materialistic way, then you will not grow so quickly, for enlightenment comes as it comes. But the purpose in pairing off is such that each will see in the other those things that they find as faults in themselves (or those things that are inadequacies). As each relates these to the other, they will learn how to overcome their own inadequacies. Remember that overcoming inadequacies and taking responsibility for yourself lead you to taking responsibility for more than yourself. And as you do so, the spirit of human-kind itself will rise.

### *There is Someone for Everyone*

Why does falling in love seem to come so easily to some people, but seems to elude so many others? It is a complicated formula, but simply put: different people make different choices. Some of us are willing to be more vulnerable, while others are not. Some are willing to easily and broadly overlook the inadequacies in another, while others are not. And some are satisfied with simple food, while others eat only gourmet. Although you may feel lonely and wonder if you will ever fall in love, understand that *everyone has another person out there* who, in opposition, perfectly matches him or her. In other words, there is always someone for everyone. Usually there are many "someones," in fact.

Finding a relationship, or love, requires several steps. If you are willing to accept that you may not perfectly match your opposite, but that the match will be close, then perhaps love can ensue. If, however, you demand an exact matching, or perfection, then you might find it very difficult, indeed, to find another who meets your standards. Like attracts like and opposite attracts opposite, but finding one who *perfectly* matches you may prove quite difficult.

In this regard, therefore, you should lower your expectations a little and be attractive yourself. Do not look for perfection first, but look for near-perfection or something that is close to being on target. Then refine it, and refine it some more, until you find someone who is exciting, and with whom you could fall in love. But *you must look;*

you cannot sit still. You must hope, for when you hope, your mind begins to attract the mind of the other. And then you must do everything you can to find that person who will become your friend, mate, or spouse. Now, there is no need for you to spend your entire day in this endeavor. But understand that when you look, you demonstrate that you are *expecting* that certain someone to walk into your life. And in doing so, you will know what you are expecting and what type of individual you are looking for. You will not form quick opinions. You will be more casual and forgiving. You will be yourself. You will allow yourself to be seen or recognized by the other. And you make clear your intentions that you are willing to pursue the other. If you wait for someone else to make up his or her mind, it may be too late.

Sometimes determination, confidence, and resolve are the factors that bring a mate into your life. But falling in love is an on-going thing. At first it is exciting: there is much enthusiasm, and your body's chemical nature physically changes. After some time, however, it becomes a matter of being able to deal with one another as you deal with all others in life: to overlook your partner's inadequacies and still have respect and consideration for your partner throughout all things. With this in mind, understand that some people *seemingly* fall in love easily. Done too easily, however, it is also too easy to fall out of love. Such individuals have a fickle nature. Those who are slow and methodical, however, seek out those who are the same: for like attracts like. There is a steady build-up towards the determination or end result, which is falling in love or being in love. Remember that, in essence, it is not a matter of how quickly or slowly you fall in love, but that you determine to *find* that person you can fall in love with. And as you continue to look, enjoy the search. When this occurs, you may fall in love rather easily and without much ceremony after all.

### *Finding a Partner*

Some people pray for love. Some people fear love. Some people don't want to give up their careers or jobs, and they put love on hold. And then there are those who expect they will never fall in love, believing themselves too ugly, or too awkward, finding fault in everything they do. Do not fear, for sometimes people are even embarrassed by those they love. Do not worry. When you come upon that certain someone who causes you to tingle and your heart to flutter, do not be afraid of affection. Rather, accept affection from all sources, for it is a very valuable commodity indeed. Explore the affection, accept it, and keep it close. Then see what your heart says tomorrow. Provided there are no obstacles or deterrents put in the way, with patience (yet determination) there is always someone who can be found for everyone. But in order to acquire love, maintain it, and keep it flourishing, it takes some effort. Be willing to make the effort. Do all you can to find love, keep love, and be in love - and you will be. Enjoy the exploration of affection. You cannot choose wrong if you always choose to accept affection.

How do you know you have found the right person for you? When falling in love takes over all of your senses. There is a joyous feeling within you for long periods of time. You become somewhat infatuated with your mate - even to the detriment of all other things in your life. Therefore, determining whether someone is right for you is a matter of enthusiasm. You may, however, also wish to assess your mate by examining his or her background, family members and even financial aspects (as well as your potential mate's romantic and physical aspects). For, indeed, to be in love is to be pragmatic to some degree: to have principles and ethics, so that when there is that chemical attraction you can give the relationship the test of time. Do not rush into things madly or boldly, for love endures forever.

To determine if someone loves you, ask yourself if he or she is courteous. Does he or she give you respect? Does he or she treat you in a preferential way? Listen with your eyes wide open, so to speak. If the answer to these questions is affirmative, then allow yourself to further explore the relationship. Be somewhat giddy, like a child with a new toy. Be in love, but be prudent. Give it some time to see if the shine on the relationship wears off. Then, do not use affection as a weapon. Do not use sex as a bartering tool. Instead, attempt to please your loved one in all ways and in all things. Your loved one will likewise attempt to please you. Then you will know that you each love the other. Observe whether or not your partner is attempting to give you as much as (or more than) you are attempting to give him or her.

When there are signs that things aren't exactly right, test your partner in some way. Do not allow doubts to manifest and prolong themselves. Without necessarily telling the most intimate of personal secrets, there should be a degree of honesty between you both. But if there is a degree of enthusiasm and desire, combined with a temperament that all things take place in their own time, then you will soon see if the relationship is a strong one, filled with love, or if it is some other kind of relationship. Give it the test of time, but attempt to make it happen with all of your mind and with all your heart. If there is no respect or simple courtesy, then you know that you have misaligned yourself. At that time, one of two changes must come about: either a change of habits, or a change of partners. But if there is love, respect, and compassion, who can say how two individuals should or should not live their lives? It is their free will and free choice, and it should be respected and tolerated by all.

## *Keeping a Relationship Alive*

In the beginning of a relationship, the two partners are in love and they are intently enthralled with one other, on all levels. They are lovers as well as friends; mates as well as spouses. They are one with each other. Throughout all cultures in the world, this concept is practiced, for it is a law of nature that two come together to be one. If this can be maintained for the entirety of your lives, then the marriage or relationship can, indeed, last and grow over the years. Strive to constantly maintain enthusiasm in your relationship. Attempt to keep it fresh, by simply paying attention to your partner, and by giving your partner little surprises time and again. In short, do not take each other for granted. Be entertaining. Be playful. Don't let the responsibilities of your lives overshadow the concept of being able to play with one another. In this way, laughter and enjoyment will always outweigh the frowns and difficulties of life.

To keep a marriage going is to share interests with each other. Strong marriages are those where the partners share activities together. The most difficult marriages are those where there is such an opposition in likes and dislikes that the two partners separate for long periods of time for their own enjoyment, relaxation, hobbies or activities. Now, both of these different paths of marriage seem to work for those who choose them. But if there can be reliance on one another, a certain degree of honesty with one other, and with each partner looking attractive for the other and desiring the other, then the marriage can be kept fresh and together. It is acceptable for a certain degree of mystery to exist between you and your spouse. But give to each other little tokens of affection - gifts of appreciation, little surprises. Know what your partner likes, and then give it to him or her, appropriately and with respect. It would be playful, and it would be meaningful. When each holds the other as meaningful and important, then each will keep the union fulfilled, the marriage strong, and affection will always be present. It does take tolerance and acceptance of each other, and a certain degree of overlooking the inadequacies and weaknesses in the other. Therefore forgiveness is a great part of marriage as well. To forgive is to be wise, for perfection does not exist in any union.

When you sense isolation, doubt, animosity, or fear, and there is criticism of each other in the relationship, you will know that it is deteriorating. For when a relationship begins to go off track, simple communication between the partners becomes filled with sarcasm, blame, and pain. It is at this point that the relationship can be aided, repaired or altered. Look for the cause, and then do something about it. Don't give up. Don't cry in the corner, wailing about something that may or may not be true. Take the bull by the horns, so to speak, and do something about it. If one partner is lazing around the house looking sloppy all day long, or not contributing to the union, what is this telling the other? A marriage is like a team of horses. One horse pulls a little harder than the other, but with a bit of manipulation of the harness, when they are matched together, they both pull evenly. As long as both partners are pulling evenly - sharing responsibilities, jobs, or duties - then there is a good chance for the union to continue. Relationships tend to go sour when there is incompleteness or when there is hardship of one spouse upon the other. But relationships are varied and different. Some couples enjoy yelling and screaming at one another, for this is their way to communicate. However, when you notice that something is going awry, don't pretend the problem does not exist. Try to determine what the problem is, and then fix it. To be patient and tolerant is good, but there comes a time when direct action is necessary. Done with love, the union may be saved. Done with negative emotions, however, and the marriage may be devastated.

## A Mate, A Friend

As well as productive, purposeful and useful, life is meant to be enjoyable. Seek to have friends, and from your friends, seek to have a mate. From your mate, seek to have a good friend to whom you, yourself, can be a good friend. There are times in life when you should be on guard, but there are also times when you may let your guard down. When you make mistakes, do not condemn yourself. When your spouse makes mistakes, do not hold it over his or her head. Learn to forgive and let the spirit of forgetfulness come into the union or the marriage. Learn to play with one another and always let laughter be in your home. For how can there be difficulty, pain and suffering, when there is laughter and joy in a household? It is the responsibility of both partners that this happens, you see; not haphazardly, as some may think.

Let your spirit soar and look for joy wherever you can find it. And then look for someone who also finds joy in the same things that you do. Pursue that person until he or she becomes your mate. If things change before there is some formal union, or if your expectations aren't fulfilled, then perhaps you should look a little further down the road. But if not, then be willing to make the commitment and the effort to pursue that person to become your mate, without shame, embarrassment, or any preconceived notion or idea. For love may be at hand, and you may not even know it. If you attempt to see in another a possibility, and you look for love each and every moment, then, sooner or later, you will indeed find that love, and you will love your mate as your mate would love you.

There are no injustices in the world. God is a loving and just God. Whether you choose to seek love, or you choose not to seek love, it is equally your right. Seek it, look for it, and when a possibility for it comes by, grasp it to find out if this is the love you are seeking. Do not be afraid of affection, fondness, or friendliness. Do not be afraid of love. For one leads to the other, and the other leads to the next.

# Chapter Sixteen

# SEX, SEXUALITY AND INTIMACY

### The Purpose of Sex

Sex is a natural function. It is an expression of affection, love or endearment. It is a union of the genders, such that as they come together, they become more than just their sum total. Usually the activities of sex are for pleasuring yourself, and indeed many people view sex simply as a pleasurable physical activity. But beyond its physical pleasure (and its procreative function), does the sex act serve some higher purpose? Certainly sex is much thought about, much talked about, and much acted upon. Certainly it insinuates itself into all the little "nooks and crannies" of the human psyche. But in the material world, physical pleasures can be a distraction. The temptation is that sex may become an all-consuming practice. At the discretion of the parties involved in the activity, sex is used for many purposes above and beyond the creation of physical life. The purpose of sex, however, is for the expression of the creative energy force. Some might call this creative energy the life force (or God), while others might call its release the Kundalini.

All physical appetites in the physical world have pleasurable aspects attached to them. Sex can be perceived as a reward, as a need for affection, or a substitute for love. A discussion of sex should differentiate between its two aspects: love and lust. With lust, the purpose of sex is individual gratification on all levels; whereas with love, the purpose of sex is the gratification of the partner. Love is an unselfish act of endearment and affection, while the other extreme is for self-indulgence. As the material world is a place of duality, therein you have the temptation and choice between two extremes. Which is it to be? Is the purpose of sex for the lustful tendencies or for the loving tendencies and affection?

Now, developments throughout your lifetime play an important part in determining which of these two sides of sex you engage in (and, thus, what the purpose of sex is). For when you are young, the driving sexual force within the body is high, and sex is expressed as the lustful tendencies. When you are older, the lustful tendencies have been gratified and expressed, and the loving or endearment aspects become more important.

As you can see, defining a single purpose of sex is difficult, for sex is multi-faceted. Ultimately the creator has given each and everyone the ability to define the purpose of sex for themselves.

### The Creative Energy of Sex

Sex is a natural desire, craving, or urging that must be met. It is a normal function that has been instilled by the creator into each and every person as a driving force so that the human race might continue. To the higher states of mind, however, sex is not merely the desire to procreate, but it is a higher form of activity. It is a function or demonstration of pleasure, endearment, and love. Those who attempt to defame, belittle or make sex repulsive are, indeed, those who are attempting to control and interfere with a normal human function. Yet there are many who attempt to control others by teaching certain attitudes towards sex. Any society which attempts to contain or control others through the emotion of guilt, or which suppresses normal functions of freedom are usually corrupt and hold back the society at large.

Sex is a very intimate and complicated function, demonstrating all the aspects of God: it can be used for the creation and propagation of the species, as an expression of great endearment, or simply for sexual pleasure or selfish tendencies. Normal sexual arousal causes this creative energy force to build up. Taken to a higher level or plane, the purpose of sex (in abstaining from it) is to take on a higher vibration of the creative force. When this creative sexual energy is allowed to accumulate in the body, is migrates up through the spinal column (or energy gateways, or chakras) and into the base of the brain. From here it continues to move upwards to the center portion of the brain to ultimately awaken the greater consciousness that emanates from the pineal gland (in conjunction with the pituitary gland). Whether it is used for physical gratification in sex, or whether it is used to empower the spiritual aspects in the physical body, this force is the source of creative energy. The purpose of sex, sexual arousal or sexual urgings, therefore, is to build up the creative force within you. How you choose to use this force, of course, is up to you.

When the creative energy is used for physical pleasure, it dissipates quickly following sexual activity. However, if the creative energy is retained through celibacy (for short or long periods), then this spiritual energy builds up within you and it can be used to express all of the creative spiritual aspects. Through denial of sexual urgings in the physical, corporeal world, you may ascend to the higher states of meditation or mind, and to the higher spiritual levels of human experience.

### The Purity of Sex

Sexual pleasure is neither sinful nor dirty, for the creator created the entire sex act. It is an urge or function that is found in nature, and nothing that is in nature is dirty or wrong. Now, lustful tendencies tend to trap you, or take you away from your natural, balanced state. As in all things, attempt to resist the temptation to indulge in anything *to the extreme*. Put limits on desires. Show some control and restraint. But as it is of the creative force, the natural urging of sexual activity is pure. The creator designed the genitals to fit together to permit coupling, so that two partners can become one. How can this be anything but divine? How can the miracle of physical life – the moment of climax when life is created – be dirty or sinful? Love-making, sexual intercourse, sex – call it what you will – is not evil. True, there is a physical appetite that must be fulfilled or addressed, but keep balanced and use some measure of self-determination and self-restraint. Do not allow this appetite to consume your life.

Sexual activity should be seen as a celebration of life and the ability to create life, not as something dirty or wrong. When experienced, it should be experienced to the fullest extent, so there are no inhibitions, no lustful tendencies built up, and no deviation from the act of affection or love. For when these tendencies are suppressed, desires appear, and desires become appetites, which must be fulfilled. As such, these appetites can turn into the outrageous tendencies of lust. In nature, each time there is "the call" (or urging, or arousal), that call must be answered. Do not allow your desires to turn into deviations or extreme behavior. For deviant or forcible sexual activity – any sexual activity that is not consensual, desired, wanted, or asked for – is sinful. This is not because the activity is sexual, but because it is the imposition of one person's will upon another. As you know, each of us possesses individual free will and free choice. To intrude upon anyone's free will or free choice is sinful. Therefore, do not allow your desire to become a perversion, for perversion leads to deviant activity, which leads to criminal or harmful activity. Desires must be met, else they become perversions or obsessions. Allow the desire to be expressed so that you will not have to meet such an extreme in the future.

### Sexualities

The cause of a person's sexuality – whether heterosexual, homosexual, bisexual or transsexual - can be understood as a combination of various forces: the person's environment; his or her biological nature; and the vibration of his or her soul. In its ultimate development, the soul comprises both genders (even though physical bodies are engendered distinctly as either male or female). As souls migrate through the various experiences or life-times in the earth, usually they tend to stick to one gender more than the other, resulting in the "mannish man" and the "woman's woman." As souls migrate towards the higher vibrations and the spiritual aspects, however, you will find that the "mannish man" becomes more of the sensitive man or the "woman's man" and the "woman's woman" becomes more of the "mannish woman" or the sensitive or demanding woman. Ultimately there would be a blending of the genders and the soul would be fully realized as one gender or the other, but perfectly balanced between the two. But as there is a crossing over from one gender to another, there can be confusion. A soul incarnating as male for the first time after a series of life-times as a female tends to have a significant amount of female tendencies. As such, this one would, indeed, have a different feeling or sense towards other males, even though it occupies a man's body. A soul which has spent many life-times as a man and then crosses over to a female body, likewise would have more "mannish" tendencies and indeed would like women more than men, because of its affiliation and previous experiences.

Those who are somewhat confused as to their gender in a biological sense — transsexuals and intersexuals — have endured some mishap in the early development of their physical body. They are somewhat of both genders or preferences. Such confusion may also result from the soul. For at the higher spiritual levels, the desire of the soul is to equally express both male and female in physical life.

For some people, sexuality is due to their biology or biological duality. For others, confusion on the soul level occurs, because of the soul's affiliation in the opposite gender for many previous experiences or life-times. Some are confused as to which gender suits them best, or which they should choose to express; while others still are equally balanced between the two of them. Regardless, it is usually the soul which determines why such qualities or such a vibration is taken on in a physical life. Whether there has been some purposeful determination to take on the body in this particular way, or whether the body is expressing such traits due to an error in biology (which is rare), it is usually the choice of the soul to experience life as homosexual, bisexual or transsexual, instead of heterosexual. A soul comes into a physical body with a variety of reasons for taking on what it would, including, to varying degrees, one gender or the other. It is up to the soul to choose what it needs to experience to fulfill its destiny. It may choose to take on the gender of one body and yet have the opposite gender be expressed. Or it may choose to close the gap between the extremes of gender, expressing both male and female tendencies at the same time in an effort to become one: physically and spiritually fully-realized. Whatever its reason(s), this is the soul's determination, and none can say what should or should not be done in the life of another.

### *The Emotions of Shame and Guilt*

Shame (and the repression of natural forces) takes you from desire into deviant activity or thinking. This does not happen immediately, but over time, when there is no expression of a desire, then resentment, guilt, self-recrimination and self-condemnation build up within. Guilt is all-consuming. It causes you to withdraw into yourself. But guilt and self-condemnation are sins. Any who condemn themselves are condemning that which is within: the soul. The soul is of God and from God. Therefore, condemnation of the self is condemnation of God.

Building up guilt only leads to greater and greater depths of despair (and, quite possibly, self-destruction). Woe be to any who accomplish this, for they will return to repeat this circumstance or uncertainty, in order to come to some understanding and self-expression, void of guilt, depression and self-incrimination. However, usually this pattern of guilt starts at a young age when some embarrassing moment occurs. An emotion is manufactured or expressed surrounding some physical or sexual aspect. This could be an admonishment from a parent, teacher, peer, or some other adult who says something offhandedly - or even purposefully – which causes deep-seated fear, guilt, and embarrassment to well up in the child. This is the starting point of guilt. However, the soul - perhaps for reasons known only to itself - has chosen to enter into this body at this particular time and under such circumstances. Perhaps it has done so in order to overcome these inadequacies, tendencies, impositions, or incriminations. For overcoming guilt is just as important as overcoming fear.

Guilt is self-manufactured. Those who are feeling guilty need to look at themselves from the outside and from the inside. They need to find in their own minds what is right and wrong, not to accept what others believe is right and wrong. Guilt is unfortunate. It may be considered a non-existent debt. Self-incrimination and self-admonishment are payments made on a debt that you did not incur. Self-destructive emotions inhibit you from fulfilling your life. They cause you to short-circuit or circumvent your life to live a less-than-joyous life - all for the feeling of guilt. The outcome of such feelings is a continued downward spiraling into darkness. However, if there is reason, understanding and self-examination, then you need not feel guilty. For guilt is usually instilled in you from someone else. In the beginning, your urging was innocent and genuine and you did not know any better (nor any worse). How can there be any wrong-doing here? To a child who is impressionable, however, the opinions of others – rightly or wrongly expressed - can change the outlook of a person (and the view of his or her nature) *for the entirety of the lifetime.* Unfortunate indeed.

## *Educating Children About Love and Sex*

Do not admonish children about their desires or natures. Do not call attention to activity that you may perceive as sexual expression, for children sometimes mimic their parents innocently. When they kiss one another, for example, they have no idea what they are doing. There is no arousal, nor is there any willful force of one child on the other. Refrain from putting your opinion on children of what is and is not acceptable if they innocently touch themselves (or others), kiss each other, hug each other, or lay on top of each other. Rather, regard this activity as a non-event. Do not call attention to it, unless there is protest from one child. Then treat the situation the same way you would when two children fight. Do not hurt them or force them to the ground. Do not imply there is anything sexual taking place. Calmly separate the children as if they were just having a disagreement over candy.

Then, demonstrate to your children that sexual activity is natural and welcome. With sexual activity comes a certain degree of responsibility. There is the responsibility of preventing unwanted pregnancy, the responsibility of child rearing, and the responsibility of relating to each other. Be honest and truthful to children so there is no inhibition or preconceived notion when the child is older. Be open and expressive to children so that, at some future time, they do not find themselves surprised or shocked that what they were taught was untruthful. Remember that children learn by example. Be the best example that you can be. Try not to show shame, but reverence for the physical body. When the time comes to speak of procreation, sexual activity, or pre-sexual activity, be honest with your child. Encourage the loving aspects of physical touch. Attempt to deal with upsetting experiences or errors openly and straightforwardly. But again, remember that children learn by example. And when your child finds him or herself in a complicated relationship, you can only state *what you would do* in this particular circumstance. Be suggestive, informative, and truthful, but also allow the child to work out his or her own problems. Therefore, be tolerant and do not intrude upon your child's life. Teach your children to be independent and teach them to understand sex as a normal function. If you do so, then you will remove the great urging and desire to discover "the unknown." This will do them a great service indeed.

### Openness About Sexuality

Generally speaking, Western society could take a page from other cultures of the world and be more open about sex. For defilement of the physical body and the implication of fear and guilt in sex as bodily sin can create two extremes in behavior. On the one hand, there is preaching against sexual activity in all its forms, in an attempt to control or regiment the biological time clock that each of us possesses. On the other, there are repressed and suppressed notions, fantasies, and desires that will ultimately manifest in later life. Those who attempt to suppress the sexual natures of an individual - or of a family, culture or society - do not do anyone a service whatsoever. For what is suppressed early in life will be expressed later on. Witness what is taking place in society today.

Instead, there should be a more open understanding about sex, but not open participation in irresponsible sexual activity. There should be tolerance and acceptance. For sex is an act that manifests or produces many emotions - jealousy, guilt, fear, anxiety, worry - as well as the most powerful of all urgings: the need to procreate. However, as there would be tolerance, acceptance, and understanding, then there can be more openness in the Western world, as there is in the rest of the world.

### *Intimacy*

To create more intimacy in your relationship, first attempt to determine ways and means to pleasure your partner. Then, seek out new ways to intimacy. Work at intimacy's different aspects, for conformity breeds contempt. When an event is predictable, it becomes boring. Put a little mystery, fun or play into your relationship. Determine ways and means to make you and your partner more fulfilled. Whether it is through romance, visual enticements, or physical touch leading to intercourse, attempt to bring newness into your relationship. Be open and honest with each other. Speak to your partner about what you desire or want, or what you desire to experiment with. Surprise each other. Change the venue. Approach each other with a state of mind that is loving, friendly and playful. Do not be robotic. Do not believe that sexual intimacy is done for duty or is part of your function as a spouse or partner. Rather, be spontaneous. Simply learn to play with each other. Learn to touch each other. Learn to hold each other. Allow feelings to develop from that point. If there is a will in both your minds, then intimacy can be embellished. But in order to do this, there must be frank and straightforward communication. Then there must be the willingness in each of you to do the bidding (or answer the request) of the other, and - provided it is not harmful - attempt to enjoy whatever is desired or requested of you.

These can be from the simplest of things to the more complex, but it all begins with communication. All too often, women complain that men do not pick up on their hints, whereas men complain they have to become mind readers to understand what women want. Women claim their partners do not pay attention to them, treating them in a predictable way, while men complain that their partners find fault in everything they do. This demonstrates a lack of communication is taking place and desired expectations are not being met. While it is nice to be pleasantly surprised, it is better to communicate what you desire. Tell your partner that you would be pleasantly surprised if this or that would be done to you. It would be much better to do so, than to go on and on complaining that your partner never gets your point, or never understands what you mean.

### *Summary*

There are volumes upon volumes that have been written on the topic of sex. Understand that no matter what, if something is done with love, it cannot be wrong. If something is done to the benefit or pleasure of your partner - as well as yourself - it would be better. If you can find a spark of arousal in all aspects of physical touch, then there will be no fear. For only without fear can there be intimacy, understanding and friendship that will go far beyond the normal function of intercourse.

Each of us has our own desires, needs, and time clock to be met. The decision to use creative, sexual energy for physical pleasure or to take it to the higher vibrations of the spiritual aspects and the development of spiritual gifts (i.e. healing and the higher states of meditation) is a personal choice. You and your partner should be tolerant of one another.

Be generous and open with one another - from the simple engaging in conversation, through all the physical aspects of touch, holding, cuddling, hugging, massaging, petting, stimulating, arousing, and so on. Let these be done with the intention of pleasuring the other and the intention of love (in all its varying degrees). This way, the sexual encounter will be fulfilling and rewarding, and it will enrich your relationship. Done with love, or the intention of love, all physical aspects of desire are not wrong.

Any physical contact should be done out of desire or pleasure, with the understanding of friendship. Doing so will help you overcome the fears, inadequacies and preconceived notions within yourself. You will not be on guard all the time, but instead, you will become open and receptive to the affection and love that God sends. To be fearful is to repel, to repel is to be isolated, and to be isolated is to be lonely. Avoid being lonely, by reaching out and seeking love. When there is some physical touch that is unwanted, do not be afraid that nothing can be done, for you have complete control and authority over your physical body, and your mental and emotional aspects. There is no need to believe that you must allow some intrusion to take place. Rather, believe the opposite: that you have the desire to meet someone to whom love can be expressed and that physical touch will be done consensually, by your own free will and accord. From the shake of the hand, to the kiss of the lips, to the merging of the genitals, each partner expresses this affection such that neither shall force their will upon the other. If this is held in your mind, then it will be fulfilled.

Remember that a kiss is not a contract for intercourse. It is simply a measure of endearment. A shake of the hand, hug or kiss does not mean there will be intercourse at the end of the day. Learn the different stages of affection so there will be no misunderstandings or unreal expectations. Above all, communicate your desires, limits, and expectations. As soon as both partners become aware and are able to do this, the game of love will be a lot easier to play. Once played, it may be played out for the rest of the life, such that old, married couples will have as much enjoyment and intimacy as newly married ones, you see.

# Chapter Seventeen

# PARENTING AND CHILD-REARING

## The Miracle of Life

Parents who are expecting a baby would do well to take steps to ensure that a positive environment is created in the household to welcome this new family member. Truly the creation of life is a miraculous thing. Prior to conception, there is an awareness that occurs on the mental levels, as the couple prays for a child. They may *earnestly pray*, they may simply *expect* nature to bring a child to them, or they may not consciously expect a baby, having doubts and reservations about their qualifications as parents. In the pre-existence, the soul chooses a physical body that will serve its purposes. Prior to conception, the soul hovers above the potential mother. It continues to do so during the development of the fetus, and throughout the birthing process as well. As such, certain alignments, characteristics, attitudes, or conditions are associated, explored, or "tried on" by the soul prior to its entering into the vehicle that the mother will provide it.

During this time, there should be some understanding, preparation, and selection of the hopes and dreams by the expectant parents for the future child. For instance, the parents could pray for a great soul to come into their lives; one who will contribute to the world and accomplish some great mission. The parents may also determine the gender of the baby they want and the type of person they hope to have in their family – whether it be a scholar, tradesperson, athlete, philosopher, preacher, teacher, police officer or soldier. In this pre-selection, what the parents hope for does not always come about. Think of it more as an advertisement to a soul of what the parents are prepared to do for their forthcoming child. In this way, parents have some free choice in their children. Now, again, it is not *always* what the parents choose that the soul assembles for itself, such as the environment, timing of the birth, the conditions that surround the birth, and even the conditions throughout its development years into adulthood. The soul of the child makes these choices for itself to suit its purposes for spiritual development. However, certain conditions can be prayed for, and to those with a spiritual understanding, they can come about.

This said, the conception of the child should be an expectation surrounded with joy, hope, and love. The mother should be surrounded with all things pleasant. The father, too, should be mindful of his contribution and association. Even as the fetus develops, it records everything that is in and about the world, including the environment, conditions, beliefs, and attitudes. While these are somewhat associated through the genetics of the child, you should be mindful of what you expose the baby to, for in the beginning it acts very much like a recording device. Therefore surround the mother with pleasant music, fragrances and sounds. The parents should strive to share, as much as possible, a peaceful, loving, hopeful and optimistic attitude – and this should be done throughout the development of the fetus, and continue even after the infant's birth. Words of love should be spoken.

Hopes and dreams should be shared with the parents about the new addition to the family. In this way, the child will be given certain influences, instincts, or a certain pattern that is conducive to the most prosperous, healthful, and productive state of mind. It is very difficult. The parents – and even those who associate with them - should be mindful of the words they use. In this way, the attitude of the child is formed or shaped, to be more evolved, correct or perfect than his or her parents. Parents should not try to make their children into something "extra-special," but they should attempt to share their hopes and dreams for their children to be greater than they are. Understand that it is an act of nature that children are more evolved than their parents, advancing past their status (or level) with the possibility for greatness. Therefore, you should expect this, and pray for this.

### *Preparing the Home*

In addition to the mental and spiritual aspects, the parents should be mindful of the physical aspects as well. The diet of the parents, and, in particular, the mother should be correct and healthy as the fetus develops. There should be no ingestion of things that pollute the body. There should be quiet and calmness in the home: a serenity that is filled with love and expectation. For this feeling or sense fills the fetus (and later, the newborn). You would be surprised at how much children retain in memory, or how well they absorb the pleasantness (as well as the adversity) that comes into their minds or consciousness during this very development-sensitive time.

Likewise, the birth of the baby should be surrounded in love. It should be calm and serene. Whenever possible, natural birth is preferable: one in which the love of the mother is given to the child immediately after the birth, and then for the next three days. During this time, you should be careful of what is said in the infant's presence or given to him or her. Even off-handed remarks, sounds or attitudes may permanently become part of the child's record. Therefore, for the first three days, surround your newborn with music, pleasant words, and as much love and support as you can give. Your baby should not be isolated, nor left on his or her own. He or she should not be allowed to become cold or feel abandoned or alone. Likewise, the baby should not be exposed to sharp sounds, loud music, or stimulants of any kind, save for those that are associated with love. For those first three days, give your baby as much positive suggestion, positive direction and support as possible. But above all, simply give love and affection, particularly in the first three days (at least). Then the parents may carry on their lives in a more usual fashion.

### Teaching Children

As it has been said, the best way to teach children is by example. Children's brains come somewhat "pre-programmed," for their curiosity and their minds are geared toward imitation. Children imitate exactly what they observe. Therefore you need not necessarily *speak* to your children to educate them. You simply have to expose yourself to circumstances and let your children observe, for they observe very quickly. It is also advisable that adults speak to children in correct adult language at all times. Baby talk should be avoided, otherwise it is as if the child learns one language and then another. Why not teach the proper language first? Now, the occasional "goo-goo" or "da-da" is fine; but at all times, attempt to speak to your child as if you are speaking correctly to an adult.

Now if a child is suppressed, coddled, or over-protected, this causes major difficulty and confusion. Attempt to teach your children the truth, whether it is the danger of things outside of the house, or the truth of a nursery rhyme. Otherwise they will face the confusion of feeling as if there is the need to undo some deception, and then discover for themselves the real truth of physical experience. For teaching children about mythical figures such as the Tooth Fairy - only later to teach that the myth is false - does teach children to be suspicious. It teaches children that parents can deceive them, and, on some occasions, it teaches them to be suspicious of everything and everyone. Therefore, feeding false information to a very delicate mind, and then informing a child at some point in time - perhaps years later - that he or she has been deceived can build up deep resentments. There are few things worse than to believe in something, only to find out that you have been willfully misdirected (or outright deceived). Making children believe in something and later revealing that the belief is a lie teaches them to disrespect authority and to make suspect all that comes to them. It also indicates to children that deception, making false statements, or misdirecting others is perfectly all right, harmless and even desirous to do. In some instances, this causes little or no notice to take place, but in others it does more harm than good. The mind of a child is a delicate thing. Be very cautious of what you put into it. The mind is the builder. The mind is the way for the person to develop, flourish, and find his or her ultimate experience while in the physical world. There are plenty of deceivers in the world. At all times, the parents should encourage trust, and trust on the word alone. That goes for the child as well as the parent.

Remember that it is how children witness their parents' reaction to things that they hold dear and near as the Truth. When a child imitates a parent, if the parent objects, this causes further confusion and disorientation, and the child has great difficulty in learning. As such, be truthful to your children, and make them aware of the dangers that are around them - but do not frighten them or give undo attention to the dangers. Simply put: the way the parents act (and react) to life and their environment is exactly what the child will begin to automatically accept as the ultimate truth.

In this way, therefore, saying one thing and doing another perplexes the inquiring mind of a child. During the first little while, this mind is a virtual recording device. Writing anything on such a clean slate (or virgin territory) is easy to do, but is very hard to erase. This thought-pattern process continues until the child reaches maximum brain growth, at about age seven. For this entire period, care should be taken on how to teach the child by example. But, again, the best way is to be honest, to explain things, and then to carry out the teachings and the explanations that you give to the child. The alternative may cause mental confusion or aberration.

### The Role of Grandparents

As the name implies, grandparents are simply additional sets of parents. Children should be surrounded with endearing love from their grandparents, as well as their parents. For the grandparents play a very important role: they are more experienced than the parents, obviously having already been parents themselves. Grandparents should exude abundant love and affection, but they should not bribe their grandchildren with gifts or toys. Nor should there be any jealousy between the sets of grandparents (or between the grandparents and the parents). They should be considerate back and forth to one other, and mindful and respectful of each other. At all times, they should respect the wishes of the parents, understanding that the parents are primarily responsible for the upbringing of the child. The lines of communication should be kept open, and the grandparents should make themselves approachable for advice (as well as the occasional baby-sitting). This should not be seen as an imposition, but rather a duty, for children who have the benefit of the extended family of grandparents will become better and stronger people when they grow up.

Therefore, the role of the grandparent should not be devalued or degraded. From the grandparent, a child absorbs wisdom; and from the child, the grandparent can absorb vitality. It is advisable for the elderly to kiss babies, for the baby absorbs the wisdom and experiences from the older person or grandparent on a subconscious level, and the grandparent absorbs some of the life-giving vitality or pure vibration of life that the child possesses.

### Encouraging a Child's Spiritual Aspects

In order to allow a child's spiritual aspects to be expressed, first of all become aware of your own spiritual aspects. Understand that when children come into the physical world, they have just made the journey from the pre-existence of the spiritual world into the physical world. It is like putting air into the tank of a scuba diver; a lot of volume is compressed into a small space. In understanding this, then you become somewhat aware that the first few years in a child's life are a transitional time. In a manner of speaking, the child has one foot in the previous existence and one foot in the present one, and, as such, he or she may remember that place from whence he or she came. If your children have invisible friends or they see a human aura (or "funny lights," or spheres in the room), do not admonish them, but make inquiry of it. "What do you see?" "What is being done?" "What does it mean?" Some people might say that the child has an active imagination. But listen to the words of your child. When you notice that he or she is not simply being inconsistent or immature, but that he or she is speaking in an adult way, you will notice a certain wisdom - even authority - come forth. At that point in time, you will know that you are directly communicating with the spiritual aspect of the child (or the soul). Then you will have a certain acknowledgement of the child's maturity. Encourage those things that the child comes to you about, and answer the questions honestly. When your child asks of the pre-existence, or says he or she can perceive deceased relatives, or claims to have some direction or advice for the family, then listen intently and see if there is wisdom in the words. When there is, you will have evidence that the child is touching upon the spiritual levels or communications, and attempting to be helpful to the family.

Become aware of the spiritual gifts, and, being familiar, you will know how to guide your child, as he or she develops them. But, again, children learn by example. Ridicule, anger, and outright proclaiming a thing to be a certain way tends to hush up and remove the subtle spiritual abilities that the child may have, become aware of, or demonstrate. It may come out in later in life, but what purpose is there in putting off opportunity for advancement to some future date? Listen to your children. They are far older and wider than many people give them credit.

## *Punishing a Child*

When children do something wrong or inappropriate, first of all, let them know how you feel. Do not conceal your feelings, nor allow them to become extreme. Next, when you consider the question of whether the child should be given some corporal punishment, consider how you would wish to be treated. And keep in mind that children are very small, and adults are very large in comparison. When at all possible, you should become as small as possible - sitting upon a chair, or on the floor – to directly communicate with your child more on his or her own level. Standing over a child, yelling and screaming is quite scary, and can cause great emotional disorders in the child. A good rule of thumb is to rationally explain to the child that something is (or is not) to be done, and why - just as you would like to know why something is or isn't. There is always a need for an explanation. Therefore, be the same with your child.

Now, when there are very great or grave behavioral problems, look for the cause. If it is not within your child, it may be within the child's world. For instance, if a child suddenly becomes ill and fearful, or is tardy or reluctant to go to school (when once he or she was very enthusiastic about school), look beyond the child to what is taking place on the way to school, perhaps, or in the classroom. Pay attention to the child's behavioral pattern, so that you might glean some understanding from it. The problem may be the child is being bullied by another pupil or a teacher, or there may be something else going on in the child's world. Therefore, constantly monitor, assess, and be aware of the child's world. In this way, giving the child attention, and letting the child know how you feel when something is done or not done, the child will very quickly have definite, clear signals of what is acceptable and what is not. This means that not only should you punish bad behavior, but you should praise the child when he or she does something right. As the pattern of behavior is continued, continue with the praise. Patterns of behavior that are not desired should be made plain to children. If a child hurts your feelings, let him or her know so. Children will repeat things from television or imitate some other person or circumstance without necessarily considering the feelings of another. Therefore you should be tolerant and overlook such transgressions, and amplify the positive aspects of a situation. Indicate that the behavior is not wanted or warranted, but refrain from admonishing the child beyond what it necessary. Refrain from embarrassing, ridiculing or outright frightening a child.

### The Need For Explanation

You should consider these the parameters of punishment for a misbehaving child. The punishment should be just and exact. Moreover, it should be *explained*. The punishment should not cause fear, nor drive a wedge in the relationship between parent and child. Always be fair and calm when you have to mete out measures of punishment. For instance, if a child throws his or her plate on the floor and wastes food, make the child aware of your disapproval. "Yesterday you threw your plate on the floor and wasted your dinner." Then take action. Do not beat, starve, or isolate the child in a small room. A more suitable punishment might be to deny the child food until he or she appreciates it. Then, explain to the child. "Obviously you don't want this kind of food, so I will not give you this kind of food. And until you want it, I will not give you food." This, then, causes the child to be active in his or her own punishment. By example, and through explanation to (and cooperation with) the child, he or she learns to correct the behavioral difficulty. The child learns that if he or she does a certain action, there will be repercussions, and there will be responsibility or accountability for the actions. This is the key for proper discipline or proper parenting of a child. Make it plain to your children that you trust them *on their word alone*, and that this trust can only be given once.

Then make it plain to your child that, as the parent, you, too, can make mistakes. When you do, take the time to apologize and explain what mistake took place. Then the child will have greater self-esteem when he or she makes a mistake, and will learn how to take responsibility and be accountable for those mistakes. All other excessive forms of behavioral discipline - beating a child, imprisonment, denial of essentials, denial of friends - need to be carefully considered. Are they teaching your child wrong things, or are they teaching correct things? Factor into this how you, as a parent, would like to be treated if you were in your child's position. Do not go on and on in explaining things. Once a behavior has been corrected or changed, there is no need to bring it up again and again - to the child's horror and embarrassment. Reward courtesy, responsibility, accountability, and the child's willingness to do his or her duty.

Finally, give your children ownership. Whatever takes place in a child's own room is his or her own business. If you find the room too messy, close the door. Do not become tyrannical, invading the bedroom and imposing your will on the child. This causes psychological difficulties in children that they may take with them for the rest of their lives. They believe they have no privacy and no responsibility to their own property or environment. Use a little reason and a little exemplification. It is far better to get a child to cooperate in his or her own punishment (or lesson) than to corporally beat or brow-beat a child. Humiliation never won over anyone.

### *Raising Good Kids in a Violent Culture*

Raising children to become people of good character starts in the beginning, and continues throughout life: by example. Children mimic the qualities of their parents. Therefore you cannot tell your children not to smoke or handle weapons when you smoke continuously or store guns and knives in the house. To raise children of good character, therefore, requires you to elevate the level of your own character first.

Do not frighten or deny your child, but do make your child aware of the dangers that exist in the world. For example, show the child what to do when the house catches on fire. Teach the child to be independent and self-sufficient. Teach the child that he or she can accomplish all things *on his or her will alone*, for the will of any person is so strong, so great, and so powerful that it is greater than all the weapons in the entire world. The negativity in the world is no greater (nor less) than it has been since the beginning. There are always difficulties. There are always choices to be made and decisions to be acted upon. Teach your child to look out for himself or herself. Teach your child to be aware. Teach your child the difference between good and bad, by example, explanation, and reason. As such, the child will learn, that, indeed, there is evil in the world. More importantly, with this understanding, your child will look for the good in the world *first*. Do not expose children to horror movies, violent television shows, or acts of murder and mayhem. Always accent the positive, and try bringing into your child's life (as much as possible) the positive aspects of life.

It is necessary, therefore, for parents to edit or protect children, by removing influences, information, or stimuli that are without merit, or that are not relevant to a child's life. If you and your children live in a mountainous area, then it becomes necessary to teach them about dangers, such as avalanches and mud-slides, and how to walk the terrain so they do not endanger themselves. Such teachings prepare children for living in such an environment, and are, therefore, positive. Likewise, if a child lives in the inner city, or some other place where there is much violence and aggression, then teach the child about the dangers of city-life outside of the home. A child will only respond to the environment that has been selected by the parent. As a parent, you have the responsibility to protect your children, but not to shelter them from the world. And, of course, you should not choose an environment that is dangerous to your children and tell them it is not. Educate and inform your children as much as possible about the environment in which they live. If you live on a farm, make your child aware that danger lurks where large animals roam freely. Teach your child about the dangers in the world that are relevant to your family, but do not place a child in harm's way. Do not frighten your children that some boogey man is going to get them, nor should you threaten that if they do something, bad things are going to happen. There is no need to go to such extremes. Simply state the facts and the reasons behind your decisions. Use common sense. Explain to your child that you want him or her to come home by 9:00 PM, because you do not want to worry that something terrible has happened. Teaching your children to be responsible for their own actions and not to be dependent or reliant upon anyone else - including another adult - is a good way to keep them away from forces of malcontent, and to go towards those things that are familiar and correct, for their own safety.

### *Advice for the Single Parent*

When a spouse is missing from a family, it is necessary to substitute someone of the same gender into the rearing of a child. A single mother needs to incorporate a father figure - an uncle, a scout-leader, a coach, a teacher, or a male friend – who can share his influence upon the child. It does not matter whether the child is a boy or a girl. Understand that a single parent cannot be both male and female, but only one parent doing both sides of the parenting. It wouldn't hurt to incorporate into the family the influence of the gender that is missing through some substitute. It is best if the substitute is a relative, but a good friend of the family is also acceptable. This helps the child learn the difference between the genders and the behavioral patterns associated with them, ensuring the proper bonding with an adult of his or her own gender. It also gives the child the ability to reach out to another adult, beyond the single parent, for single parents tend to be (or try to be) a friend first, and a parent second. This can be a little confusing to children. A child should have the influence of more than one adult source at this intimate level. For even the daughter of a single mother needs to have another female figure in her life: whether she is an aunt, a grandmother, a teacher, or a coach. The more adults in a child's life, the better.

### *Investing in Your Own Future*

Bringing children into the world is a fairly long commitment: a life-long one, in fact. But understand, how you treat your children when they come into the world, and how you show, teach and speak to them in their formative years will come back to you when you are old. When your children are adults - and you are a mature, older adult - they will give back to you the exact same behavior as you gave out. Not one iota more or less. Consider this when you teach your child something. Look at your child as an investment in your own future. Love your child with all your love, for someday the child will have control over you, as presently you have over him or her.

Understand that a child is an addition to a family. A child adds to the relationship of the parents, and does not detract from it, nor does a child divide or distract the couple. Love your children. Encourage them always. *Show them*, for children only learn by example. Give your children responsibilities. It is your duty that they will live up to the responsibility that they have taken (or which you gave them). Befriend your children. Teach them by example. Give them respect and reverence and they will give it back to you. If a child becomes a problem, let the child work out the problem for himself or herself. Be supportive, but at all times make it plain that your child has to live his or her own life. As parents, you have but a short time before you must let go - and let go you must. Therefore, always teach your children to be independent and self-sufficient. For if you teach dependency, then you are failing your children. But if you teach independence and self-reliance, when your children make errors in life, they will know that the errors were made through free will and free choice.

Do not take responsibility for your child's mistakes in life. It is acceptable that your children face a little adversity and difficulty. But be the parent. Be the best parent you can be. Be ever willing to be the best parent you can be. Ask everyone how to be a better parent, but it is your example. It is how *you* treat your children that is the most significant. When you make a mistake, therefore, apologize to your children. When you do not make a mistake, allow them to live up to become what they originally intended to become. Your children wish to allow their spiritual aspects to come out of their physical forms, so that they might understand the greater consciousness. Encourage them. Guide them. Help them to raise their own level of consciousness to the greatest level while in the physical world. When you look at a child, look carefully and you will see genius.

# Chapter Eighteen

# SUCCESS AND PROSPERITY

Success is something that is measured by many benchmarks. Some say success is the acquisition of money. Some say success is the acquisition of status, privilege, rank or authority. Some say success is living a very peaceful and contented life. And there are others who say success is jumping over a riverbank. Success is very personal. The best explanation of success is that it is the ongoing working towards a worthwhile goal or endeavor, and then achieving it. It is participating in some project and accomplishing some end. Success, therefore, includes four things: the commencement of a purpose or ideal; the building, constructing or manifesting of it; the ultimate acquisition or completion of it; and then the receiving of rewards or gain from the initiative. Success is, therefore, both in the doing and in the acquiring, and in doing so, harvesting some gain or some excess from the initiative.

### The Key to Success

The first and foremost key to success is the determination to become successful. Once this has been decided, and it is held in your mind without doubt, reservation, contemplation of failure, or thoughts that would divert you from the end result, then you will have success. The first step, therefore, is to remove any doubt, worry, concern, or notion that your success will not be achieved. If you become desperate to acquire or achieve success, then you will achieve it.

Second, understand that success must be a singleness of purpose. If you were a hunter, hunting the greatest game – such as an elephant - and you used a shotgun to hunt your prey, you would scatter your energies hither and yon. A successful elephant hunter, on the other hand, uses a rifle, concentrating all of his energies into one direction or one source. He would, indeed, capture the greatest game, and achieve success. Success, therefore, might be considered as putting your mind to it. In other words, your mind should not be distracted, nor misdirected. For success is a journey from Point A to Point B. There is no in-between. There is no going in several different directions. Success is a series of objectives, in a particular order, which allow you to go from the beginning, through the middle, and to the end. If your objectives can be clearly seen - and if they are tangible - then you can go through the objectives, knowing and measuring how far you have gone, and how close you are to your ultimate goal (or to your success). Achieving success, therefore, is a series of accomplishments from one objective to the next, with a clear and definite goal at the end of the line.

### The Process of Success

In your mind, success must be not a condition (like "being happy"), but it must be something tangible: a definite goal. A goal is finite. A condition is not. For how do you know when you are happy? Some people might say, "When I have one hundred dollars in my bank account, I will be happy." Happiness, of course, is the end result of acquiring the funds and putting them in the bank. To reach this goal, the objective could be to put one dollar a week into the bank account. Then there could be a weekly measure of the accomplishments to see the growing direction towards success. In this way, one can also know when one has arrived at the goal or the success. In this example, there is a clear, tangible goal that can be seen or (in the material sense) realized. Feeling happy about accomplishing the goal is the condition. Be careful not to confuse the condition with the goal. You cannot constantly aim for the condition and forget about your goal. Conditions are only brought about *after* a goal has been acquired or achieved. Your happiness is the result of something else taking place or being achieved.

Acquiring success, then, is a process. You must have a lot of little successes along the way to acquire the big success. Little successes are acquired by objectives, and the objectives are laid out as a plan to be followed and not deviated from (save for compromising or altering the plan, if need be). It is like planning a vacation. First a choice is made - for example, "Let's go to Hawaii." There is some knowledge of what Hawaii is, and there is some desire, motivation, or reason for going to Hawaii. What follows is a series of decisions or choices geared towards physically getting you to Hawaii. You need to make preparations, such as what belongings you will need for your trip. You need to plan your hotel accommodation. You need to orchestrate a complete schedule of transportation - from your home to the airport, to the airplane, and then from the airport in Hawaii to your hotel. Once at your hotel room, your belongings safely stored, you will then carry out the activities that you had planned to do on vacation. Only then will you know that you have achieved your goal: you have been successful in making the trip to Hawaii. No doubt, you would be happy, because you are there and have attained your objective.

The elements of achieving success in life are the same as those in planning a simple trip. You must first gather knowledge, experience, or education in order to propel yourself forward in the present moment to your distant or future objective. You cannot, therefore, become something of which you have no knowledge or experience. In order to acquire some success in the future, you must acquire knowledge or experience now. All success in the future is built upon your ever-expanding past.

So, first is the determination to become successful. Second, is the will to follow through to acquire the success. Many people get to the threshold of success, but they are afraid to take that one, last step. Others are deterred from success because they deem it too difficult (not realizing that success is just another step away). It can be said, therefore, that successful people are somewhat "marked," for they complete what they start. Their expectations in the beginning may be different than the realizations at the end, but they complete what they start, and therefore - to the greatest degree - they become successful. It does not matter whether they score a one out of ten or a ten out of ten, for they have completed what they started and, therefore, they are successful; sometimes more successful, and sometimes less, but always successful, nonetheless.

### Tenacity

With this understanding, and by following these steps, you can easily become successful - but it must be with tenacity. When problems arise, solve the problems. When difficulties or challenges arrive, do not be discouraged, deterred or dissuaded. Be tenacious. Follow through to the very end. Most importantly, however, try not to judge yourself while you are between the beginning and the end. Only at the very end can you judge whether or not you have been successful, for only then will you have the knowledge, experience, and authority to make such a judgment.

As such, it might be considered that success is simply the willingness to make decisions and the tenacity to follow through on those decisions. It does take a little foresight to do this, and this comes from the experience and knowledge in your past. Put this into practice and you can achieve what you set your sights on and acquire the largest gain. No matter what it is, or how long it takes, as long as there is a driving desire to acquire your goal, you will be successful - and, in fact, you have been successful right from the moment you began.

### Success vs Failure

Failure is a sense of giving up. When you give up in your mind, it is only a matter of time before you give up in your body or in the physical world. Success is a choice. You can make decisions that lead you to becoming a success, or you can make decisions that lead you to becoming a failure. A drug addict or alcoholic living on the streets can be considered a very successful person, since he or she made every decision correctly in order to become such a person. Had he or she made every opposite decision, then he or she would have been a failure at being someone on skid-row, and instead would have been a wealthy entrepreneur (for instance). There is no difference between these two extremes, save for making a particular decision. In one instance, all of the decisions to get to the lowest end of society have to be made; whereas in the other, the reverse of each decision must be made to get to the other end of society.

To a great degree, tenacity is the difference between a success and a failure. Generally speaking, usually people who are failures are not tenacious. Another way of putting this is that *successful people always do the things that failures are afraid to do*. Tenacity is overcoming uncertainty, fear, worry, and doubt - as well as the objectives and opinions of others. Often it has been said, "Tell no one your prayer," meaning that you should tell no one your real intentions or your goals. At the outset, keep those things that are personal to you quiet or secret, else another's doubt or jealousy may affect the delicateness of the thought in your mind. By keeping your goal secret, not only are you able to skirt the doubters, objectors, and detractors, but your thought is also allowed to manifest into something strong.

Why are successful people tenacious? Because they *expect* to gain, they *expect* to be successful, and they *expect* to accomplish things. They are not afraid of work. They are not afraid of doing difficult things. They are not afraid of doing things on their own. They do not defer to someone else and get another opinion of whether or not they should do something. They assess the situation and make a decision. If it is wrong, they correct it and move on. If it is right, they continue to the next decision. This is the difference between a success and a failure. The successful person always does the things a failure is afraid to do.

When you become desperate – say, for instance that your house on fire - there is no doubt what you should do. There is an order of events that must be done, and the events must be done sequentially, quickly, and decisively. You do not consider anything else when your house is burning down. Whether it is calling the fire department, waking up the family members, rescuing the family photos or your prized possessions, or grabbing a fire extinguisher and trying to extinguish the fire yourself; whatever you do, you instantly have a plan and a process in your mind, and you are tenacious at attempting to accomplish your goal. But the order of decisions makes you more or less successful at putting out the fire. Therefore, the willingness to make decisions (and also the willingness to experiment or make mistakes) is indeed a stepping-stone to success. Mistakes can be corrected. The willingness to make a mistake is, indeed, the willingness to learn. The willingness to learn automatically leads you to becoming more successful.

### *Prosperity*

Generally speaking, to become more prosperous in your life, figure out ways and means of being of greater service to others. Then give the best service you possibly can. Work as if your life depended upon it: as if you were working for God. And in giving the best service you can, expect to be well paid in return. The giving of service is a fundamental of prosperity. The amount of money you make is the yardstick, meter, or indicator of how much service has been offered, used or accepted. If you are attempting to offer some service that no one wants, you will not be of much service. Therefore, your financial gain – the barometer of your service - will not change. But if you become of greater service, giving the best that you possibly can, and giving service that everyone wants and needs, then you will soon see yourself becoming very successful and very prosperous. Whatever it is you desire to gain - money, fame, accommodation, or material assets – you will gain. A rule of thumb, therefore, is: figure out ways and means to be of greater service, give the best service you possibly can, and expect to be well paid. Then you will gain in prosperity.

Enthusiasm is the indicator or barometer to judge what type of work is best suited for you. Many people do things they like for little (or no) monetary gain, while others work very hard at things they detest. While they gain monetarily, they are not in harmony, and life is difficult. If you wish to, find out something that you love to do (or like to do). If you direct yourself towards this end, you will never work a day in your life again, for you will be occupying your time with enjoyable "play-time" activities that are productive and fruitful. In doing so, you will find great purpose and accomplishment as well. Enthusiasm, accomplishment, and personal satisfaction are the indicators that you should look for in the vocation, work, or career for which you are suited. As long as there is desire towards accomplishment - and there are accomplishments - then your purpose can be determined, felt, or seen. With enthusiasm, you become very self-loving, self-confident and full of pride, and, in this regard, become more successful.

### Choosing a Career

Sometimes young people choose to train themselves into a certain discipline, career, or job. There is nothing to say they cannot change careers in mid-stream, if they feel they have made the wrong choice. For staying with a job that causes you worry and anxiety or is disgusting, meaningless, or arbitrary to you is a waste of your life. As it has been said, "If thy right arm offend thee, cut it off." In all occupations, there are difficulties. Learn to do what you love, and when the disappointments, hardships, problems or concerns arise, you will meet them with the same optimistic and enthusiastic outlook as you would in overcoming some dilemma in any other project or game in life.

In order to go into a particular career or vocation, you must first educate yourself, or become experienced in something. You cannot start from nothing and become something. Do a self-analysis to determine what you are best suited for. What are all the things you like to do? What are all the things you are trained to do? What are all the things you are very good at doing?

Consider this example. A man is trained to be a train engineer, but his real passion is model-building. He hates the long trips at work and the time away from home. He is sick. He is angry all the time. He and his wife plan to take the family on vacation "some day," but it never gets done. Why does he do this? What keeps him on a job he detests? The money. If he were to turn his model-building hobby into a vocation, perhaps his finances would be less. But, perhaps they would be more. What is assured is that he would be doing something he loves. His lifestyle would be greatly different in doing what he loves to do, rather than doing what he detests. His home life and his family life would be better. A sense of peace and enjoyment would have been acquired and maintained. More than likely, he will live longer and have a more enjoyable life. As he is playing at this activity more than working, he would become a supreme model railroad builder. And perhaps he would become such an expert in model railroads that any who desire to become knowledgeable would beat a path to his door. His prosperity would automatically increase. He would become successful, knowing that this is what he is best suited for.

Knowing what you are suited for is a daily choice. If you find yourself hating your activity, then change. Change for the sake of your soul and for the harmony and peace that should be in your life. Find whatever it is that you love to do. Find out what brings enthusiasm into your life, such that you can hardly wait to get up the next day to do it. Then you will know that you have chosen correctly. If you have not chosen, then make arrangements to find what you wish to do. Acquire the knowledge and the experience necessary, and then commence in all practical ways. Be prudent in the transition to do work that you have chosen to do, rather than doing what has been chosen for you, or what you have haphazardly come to be employed in.

### *Material Wealth*

It is not wrong at all to want material wealth and large sums of money. God, the creator and giver of all things, is like the ocean. The abundance of the ocean is such that when you go to the ocean, you may take as much as you want. Whether you go with a tea-cup or a tanker-truck is your choice. It makes no difference to the ocean. Material wealth - or material excess - is both a matter of choice and of lifestyle. If you believe you do not need any material wealth, ask yourself why you are reading this book and not standing nude in the middle of a forest somewhere? If, on the other hand, you believe you *do* need material wealth, then understand that you have already obtained clothing, shelter and food for yourself. You are supporting yourself, paying your bills, and you are attempting to acquire more material wealth to sustain yourself and your family. Those who do not have material wealth cannot help anyone; not even themselves. Those who have material wealth, however, help themselves. And those who have material wealth *in excess* are able to help themselves as well as those who cannot help themselves, or who are not as fortunate.

Therefore, let your prayer be for plenty, for plenty is of God. Does God not give all things to everyone in the world? Consider God as that force that creates the harvest. A farmer may plant a seed in fertile ground or soil, but it is God that makes life come into the seed, the seed to turn into a plant, and the plant to bring forth more than what was started with: plenty.

The acquisition of material wealth is, therefore, part of the birthright of everyone. Whether one chooses to live on $50.00, $500.00, $5,000.00, or $500,000.00 a week is totally up to the individual. Remember each of us possesses our own free will and free choice. It is wrong to interfere with (or steal) the free will and free choice of anyone. To gather great sums of wealth or great material abundance is neither wrong nor sinful. Those who horde wealth, however, and those who see material wealth as their God, are unfortunately misguided. You should feel a little sorry for these poor, misguided souls, for material wealth is little more than a temporal thing. Everything that comes into one hand eventually leaves by the other. All material wealth or material excess will come to pass. Understanding and controlling material wealth is, indeed, a skill itself. But realize that all things – including abundance - come to pass. Do not succumb to the temptation to allow money to become your God or the driving force that isolates you from all other aspects of life. Money is a false God.

God is the great creator and giver of all things. Whether you want a cupful or a tanker-truck-full is your personal choice, but you must be willing to make the effort. It does not take much effort to take a tea-cup down to the ocean. It does take a little more effort to acquire a truck, learn to operate it, get it to the ocean, and have the willingness and the time necessary to fill it up. But through this struggle, or through this plan of acquisition, the reward is much greater, is it not? If you desire it, then make the effort.

### Material Wealth and Spirituality

Some people question whether it is possible to be both wealthy and spiritually-minded. The answer, of course, is yes, for many who are wealthy find themselves taking care of their brothers and sisters (i.e. their fellow humans). In having wealth, one not only takes on responsibility for oneself, one then begins to take on responsibility for others (and ultimately for the entire society). Bear in mind that if you are impoverished, you cannot help anyone else, for you are having difficulty helping yourself to begin with. But those who have acquired great wealth must take responsibility in handling it. Like all things in nature, money is, indeed, a resource or energy that must be handled correctly. Handled incorrectly, it dissipates and flees out of the hands of those who cannot control it, and into the hands of those who can.

Even the greediest person who hoards money in the bank does an awful lot of good, for the stored money is loaned out as mortgages to other bank customers. Used in this way, the money allows other families the ability to buy their own homes. In order for this to be accomplished, a wealthy individual is needed to supply the material wealth, and in this way, the responsibility belongs directly to him or her. Others who are wealthy give to society in a more direct way. In doing so, the wealthy participate in the welfare of their fellow human beings, their neighborhoods, their cities, and the welfare of the world

(and as much as they help others, they benefit themselves). This, therefore, is God's work.

Therefore, pray for abundance. Pray for all aspects of God: health, wealth, and peace of mind. For health is, indeed a wealth; it is the wealth of the body. Health is important to all aspects, for a healthy mind and body allow for the healthy expression of the spiritual tendencies (or the spiritual self).

The world is a place of great abundance. It is not possible for anyone to own all the wealth in the world. Now, many have a tendency to flee from wealth, hiding in austere temples, buildings, or mansions for fear of being tempted by the excess of material things. This is not the spiritually correct way. Live in the world. Allow yourself to be tempted. Do show restraints in these temptations and be moderate in all you do. For the sin of the rich is gluttony. The wealthy can afford rich foods, and when taken to excess, these take a toll on the body. You can, of course, eat rich foods and enjoy the best the world has to offer without committing sin. However, it takes discipline to place limits on desires. Therein lies a key to success, abundance, and wealth.

First, decide to have the very best. When you acquire it, do not abuse, misuse or over-use what you have acquired, but revere it and respect it. This is a demonstration that you have a limit on your desires. Financial freedom is sometimes used as a yardstick for success, but financial freedom is little more than being able to choose what you would do without worry of tomorrow or financial hardship. In each and every day look at how much money you need. Usually people think they need more than they actually do.

In itself, money does not exist. It is a false God. Yet, money is something that people pray for night and day, every day of the year, all around the world. Instead of money, let your prayer be for plenty. Let your prayer be to God Almighty. Let your prayer be for opportunities, for people to bring you those opportunities, and (most importantly) for the knowledge to recognize when an opportunity - or person bringing an opportunity - is at hand.

### Summary

Let your body and mind be disciplined. Temper your emotions - which are the constructive and destructive forces in your body. Do not be afraid to be successful. Be willing to step out of step, not locked into conformity (which is usually the formula for failure). If you step outside of the ordinary and routine, there is a good chance you are falling upon new steps that will lead you towards success. Over ninety per cent of people are failing. In the Western world, most people at age sixty-five are penniless and totally dependent upon someone else for their livelihood. About three to five per cent are comfortable and able to manage on their own resources and their own acquisition of income. Somewhere between one and three per cent of the population are, indeed, truly wealthy. They do not need to rely upon anyone for their creature comforts and needs, for they have managed to save up, produce, gain, or acquire money throughout their lives. This has brought them into a state of being wealthy.

Anyone in society can do the same. First, and foremost, it takes a good understanding of money management. Second, it takes the ability to acquire material excess, or more money than you think you need. Third, it takes some degree of management of these resources. And fourth, it takes an attitude that what you are doing in your vocation or career is something you love to do. In the end, you become self-empowered, self-determining, and self-successful and you need not depend on anyone for your future sustenance. You depend on yourself and God - which is a loving and just God - for your ultimate success.

Each and everyone can acquire success. When in doubt, when feeling self-pity, or when worry or fear holds you back, it is better to do something – *anything* - than nothing. Be willing to take the first step, and do anything you can to become self-supporting. Look for answers under all possible avenues. Do not stop until you find the right answer and you will find that you have gone from despair to delight; from darkness to light. The rules are simple: choose what you want to become, but be willing to make compromises, changes or shifts in direction. Do not stop the ongoing desire to acquire your ultimate success. Let your ultimate success be something tangible; something that can be measured in physical terms. Then, every minute of every day, do everything in your power to acquire that end result or that goal. Do not be dissuaded or discouraged. When you fall down, get up. When you feel delay, continue. Reach out and reach your goal. No one else will stop you. No one else will do it for you. Just like breathing, success is a personal thing. Continue to breathe. Continue to be successful. Continue to be self-determining and self-supportive.

Learn to be wealthy. Speak to the experts. As you move through life, use your own understanding. If you are usually doing something different than everyone else, then you must be doing something right, for conformity is a sin. Conformity keeps you limited, isolated, and unwilling to expand. Do not conform. Utilize the rules and regulations, but do not conform.

# CHAPTER EIGHTEEN

Success is at the hands of all. Choose what you will choose for yourself, though light, life, success and prosperity seem the better choices. Enjoyment of all things in the world is part of the human experience - your privilege, if you will - while you are in the flesh. Do not let material things deter you from your ultimate success. Rather, learn to use them to acquire it. But never substitute material wealth or material prosperity as the true God. God is a loving and just God. Love God with every cell of your being. Always do what is right, and you will be successful. No matter what.

## ABOUT THE AUTHOR

*In the mid-1970s, Douglas James Cottrell learned to develop his innate intuitive abilities by harnessing the power of the contemplative mind. Over the years, he has counselled thousands of people the world over who have sought his insight and guidance on such varied topics as health, relationships, and commerce. Because of his special ability to articulate complex spiritual matters in plain language, Douglas is most often compared to Edgar Cayce, the best-documented genuine intuitive of the Twentieth Century. A renowned speaker, instructor and advisor, Douglas has contributed to a variety of publications, including* Psychic Guide *and* Body Mind Spirit *magazines. This is his first book. Douglas lives in London, Ontario, Canada with his wife, Karen. They have four children.*

## ABOUT THE EDITOR

*Having been exposed to his father's work all of his life, Douglas M Cottrell has a unique perspective on spiritual abilities such as precognition as well as the laws that govern the spiritual dimensions. A graduate of the University of Western Ontario, where he earned a Master's Degree in English, Douglas has worked as editor on a number of consumer health publications, including* Energy *magazine. He lives in London, Ontario, Canada.*

www.douglascottrell.com